DAUGHTER

EMBRACING THE DIFFICULT JOURNEY OF CARING
FOR A DYING PARENT WITHOUT FALLING APART

LAURA DILL

Cover Design: Jennifer Stimson

Editing: Cory Hott

Author Photo Credit: Ania Scheiman

ADVANCE PRAISE

"You can feel Laura's entire soul rooting for you as you flip the pages of *Daughter*. No matter the stage in caregiving you are in. She sees you. She hears you. She validates you. She's got you and makes you feel you've got this."

— JESSICA, LOVING AND CAREGIVING
DAUGHTER WITH A BIG-HEARTED SOUL

"As Laura Dill takes you through the unthinkable and heart wrenching journey of losing two parents at the same time, she somehow brilliantly weaves a story of resilience, strength, and tenacity. She expresses beautifully the fierce, fierce love of her family carrying her through with the sheer determination of creating a foundation to help those suffering the same unimaginable fate. Laura, her heart, her story, and the SLAY Society are pure gifts. She shows us we can indeed do things we never thought possible."

— BILLI J. MILLER, AUTHOR

"Laura takes you on her emotional journey as she deals with the unimaginable – simultaneously caring for both parents with the same terminal cancer. You will get swept up by her emotional roller coaster and learn of the often-overlooked ripple effects that touch more than just the caregiver. If you are a caregiver, *Daughter* will set you up for success as Laura shares the lessons she's learned along the way. For everyone else, it's impossible not to be moved by Laura's story and resiliency. A page-turner from the start. Definitely a must-read."

— KRISTY CHAPMAN, POSSIBLE FUTURE
CAREGIVER, AVID BOOK DEVOURER, MOM OF
THE YEAR, AND BEST FRIEND FOR LIFE

"Laura bounced back from the unimaginable, not only surviving but thriving in her role as caregiver. Let this amazingly powerful story and helpful book be your guide so you, too, can rise above."

— COLLEEN CANNON, FORMER CAREGIVING
DAUGHTER, LOVER OF ALL HUMANITY, AND
SOUL SISTER

"Laura's resiliency shines throughout *Daughter*; and the wisdom within removes the guessing work on how to do caregiving with integrity and grace and without the pain of regret. This work serves as a profound testimony of how we can become empowered to transform our deepest pains in life into our greatest purpose to serve with a passionate and gracious heart – a true testament to the power that lies deep within all of us. Anyone embarking on the seemingly impossible journey of slaying the ultimate dragon (being a daughter and caregiver while simultaneously wearing multiple other hats) will benefit from the lessons of determination, resiliency, and raw vulnerability offered within this collection of divine wisdom."

— NICOLE ZAYHOWSKI, FORMER CAREGIVER,
GLIOBLASTOMA SUPPORT GROUP
ADMINISTRATOR, BS/CMT/LMT, AND EMPATH
EXTRAORDINAIRE

CONTENTS

To my parents, Gerry and Christine, who taught us that the best way to slay a dragon is to laugh in its face.
Your light will continue to shine all over this great big world – I will make damn sure.
I will miss you until the day I find you again. Please never stop visiting me in my dreams.

FOREWORD

Seven years ago, I was faced with impossible news. My mom had just been diagnosed with stage-four lung cancer and there was little that could be done in the way of treatments. Besides that, my mother chose to not take the chemotherapy that was offered. My role as a daughter was forever changed when I became my mother's caretaker and medical advocate.

This was before my death doula training. Although I had healthcare experience and I could navigate the medical side of what was happening with my mom, I was at a loss when it came to everything else.

Like Laura Dill, I found myself in a position that I never asked to be put in – caregiving for my dying parent. Through the process, I learned that my mom had been planting seeds of knowledge my whole life that would support me as I supported her through the end of her life.

When I read Laura's book, *Daughter*, I was transported back to that time and could see clearly how her words would have brought me comfort by showing me that I was not alone in taking care of my mother, that I could find beauty in the hard moments, and that I could take small steps to provide care for myself. When I learned of my mom's terminal illness, the way time moved changed. Everyday tasks that had been necessary before diagnosis became stupid or not worth the effort. There was nothing like a terminal illness to show me what was truly important in my schedule, and it was not what I was spending most of my time on. I stripped away many of the everyday routines that became time wasters during my time as a caregiver.

In doing that, I also lost some of the routines and self-care practices that I needed to continue to endure what my family was going through. But I had time for a book like Laura's. I had time for the mindset she teaches and the simple actions she encourages caregivers to take. *Daughter: Embracing the Difficult Journey of Caring for a Dying Parent Without Falling Apart* is a book that caregivers should make time to read. It is full of simple actions that you can take when faced with the impossible situation of losing your family member.

Now, years after my mom's death and being a death doula, I can tell you that the simple steps Laura lays out in *Daughter* will help you support your loved one even on the days when you are questioning your ability to do so. Not only that, but she also gives you permission to request as a caregiver to become a part of your family member's medical care team.

In reading Laura's story and putting yourself in her experience. You learn that a dying or sick person's care team does not need to be just made up of medical professionals; family, friends, and community members can all support the dying person in big and small ways.

In reading Laura's book, you will find the courage to dig deep and show up for your loved one in an intentional way all while allowing yourself to be sad, mad, and all the other emotions that show up in this complicated experience. You will also get to know Laura's parents and the seeds of knowledge and leadership that they planted throughout her life that nurtured her ability to not only caregive for them in their dying times, but also for her to caregive you as you go through your journey. Laura is the caregiver's champion.

— KELLY RUBY HANSON, DEATH DOULA,
CERTIFIED SURGICAL TECHNOLOGIST, AND
AUTHOR OF *DEATH DOULA: TOOLS AND
TECHNIQUES FOR END OF LIFE SUPPORT*

PREFACE

Just like that, I was back in the hospital's long, yellow corridors. The experience was unplanned and unwanted, yet everything I needed. It felt like the time since I had last been there had been nanoseconds and eons in equal measure. The familiarity enveloped me with dread and anticipation. To describe the feeling in my heart and stomach as conflict was a grand injustice to the turmoil bubbling inside of me. Those faded murky yellow walls, again, offering a grim reminder that most people who entered this hospital would never leave. It smelt like a combination of antiseptic and human excrement. Bile rose in my stomach at the thought of how I was going to tell her he was gone. How would I keep myself from falling apart?

The hospital's chaplain followed behind me to ensure I did not stray from the deliberate and militantly laid-out direct path from the front door to my mom's room. Ducking out was no longer an option. Thirty minutes was all I was being gifted.

I was clad in my usual mid-shin-length, yellow, papery gown. The strings of my N-95 mask were tight against my cheeks and already leaving lines that I knew would serve as a reminder that this had happened for hours after it had. They chafed the backs of my ears and I had not even made it to her room. The latex gloves stuck and squeaked between each of my sweaty fingers. A full plastic face shield ran the length from my forehead to my collarbone.

My mom was asleep when I got to her door. I could only see the back of her head from the position of her bed. I was startled by the stark white circle of newly revealed scalp created by shedding hair even though I had only been away for nine days. She was as still as could be. Her television hung high in the corner and blared loudly in the background – *Three's Company*. Her usual muse that maybe did not muse her at all anymore, but we always had them turn on the show for her for comfort.

As I walked around to the front of her bed, I willed her head to move. I lumbered with great noise due to the cumbersome nature of my swishing, squeaking armor. There she lay, my beautiful, sweet mother, only sixty-three years young. The noise I made did not rouse her. I could feel my heart beating hard against the inside of my ribs. I could feel the bile rising again. I could feel myself consciously trying to swallow it down. As nauseous as I felt I could not risk spending my now twenty-seven minutes vomiting on my dying mother and cleaning it up. Besides, she had usually been covered in enough of her vomit.

Nothing I did would wake her. It occurred to me then that she could be gone. Was it possible to lose both parents on the same day? I grounded myself and called her name loudly. I squeezed her bony hands and watched her chest rise and fall ever so faintly. I exhaled a sigh of defeat. Nothing was rousing her. Glioblastoma brain cancer could induce a sleep deeper than any meditative state could ever achieve. I cried from somewhere deep within the place where I had stuffed the volcanic bile. The cries were guttural. They hurled me forward with each noisy exhale. I wailed for her to open her eyes – to see me, to hear me, to be mom again. After nearly twelve straight minutes – leaving eighteen minutes of visiting time – she did.

Her dull grey eyes once shone as bright as emeralds. Now they just stared vacantly. Not into my eyes, she had lost the ability to do that – to see me. Instead, she looked at, past, and through me all at once. And while my heart knew that her heart and mind felt differently and were overshadowed by her damaged brain, my head could not see past the vacancy in her eyes and the straight line of her mouth, unperturbed by my presence.

I tried to talk but just shook. The sounds that followed were little broken pieces of syllables punctuated by deep sniffles. I had to find the strength to tell my mom that my dad had just died, only hours before, by the same brain cancer she was about to die of too.

Nearly twelve hours earlier I woke from a staccato sleep at a different hospital across the city. I had been spending most nights there sleeping on an uncomfortable hospital chair beside my dad who had been unconscious for nearly nine days. We were participants in a long and excruciating waiting game until his last breath. At 2:00 a.m. that morning I woke and watched for the faint expansion of his ribs. Oh good. He was still with us.

When I woke again one hour later for my usual hourly check, I was met with only stillness. No rise. No breath. No life. I froze.

We could only have one family member with him at a time and nurses would not touch me with a ten-foot pole, even armoured in personal protection equipment (PPE). I stood there in the cold and dark, completely alone with his body.

After heading home later that morning and managing several hours of staring at my ceiling, I was awarded the opportunity to go tell my mom of his passing in person. I did not want it. I hated it. I needed it.

Back in my mom's room I sobbed and snorted as I blurted out to her with no eloquence whatsoever that he was gone. I held the guilt of being the messenger, the utter pain of seeing her in this state, the heart searing reality that after these thirty minutes I would not be allowed back to see her for the foreseeable future due to a global pandemic, and the disgusting unmentioned understanding that she was inevitably next.

YOU CAN DO THIS

There was something about my mom's text that made all the hairs on the back of my neck spike. She never texted me. She always called. It could have been the curt tone or sense of urgency. The top right corner on my phone told me that it was 9:12 a.m. This seemed uncharacteristic as she should have been at church already. It was Sunday morning, the day after my thirty-seventh birthday. My cousin Jamie had just arrived at 9:00 a.m. for an early morning birthday coffee catch-up when my phone lit up on the kitchen table in front of me.

My mother was a devoted Christian who never missed a Sunday service. *Weird*, I thought. There was no way she would be texting me in church. The text read, "Are you available for a chat? I have a lot to tell you this morning."

This may not have sparked a tingle down the spine of anyone else, or if it had come from anyone else, but I knew my mom well. She always called me "Kid." She never started a conversation with a direct question this way.

I excused myself from the table and my cousin, got my

coffee, went up to my bedroom, closed my door, and hit the phone icon. I immediately felt nauseous. I could not handle more bad news after what had just happened to our family.

Exactly fourteen days earlier, on a hot, humid day in August, we celebrated my daughter Ryann's seventh birthday in our backyard with a big family barbeque. My parents divorced when I was seventeen but were strong and level-headed enough to navigate the waters of a broken family and split custody with grace. When important dates came along such as graduations, weddings, and then grandchildren, it was never any question that they would all be there, new spouses included, without so much as a second thought. We were blessed to watch my children grow up with grandparents that no longer seemed as broken as my brother and I once knew them to be.

I watched my fresh-faced seven-year-old skip and giggle in the backyard with her brother and sister while my parents, stepparents, in-laws, aunts, and uncles all cheered her on. But while I rejoiced in the warmth that was watching every part of a once torn tapestry weave itself back together with the common thread of grandchildren, my head could not ignore the growing concern for my dad's health.

In the previous few months, he had changed. He was a well-respected, quick-witted, successful accountant whose sharpness was fading. His smile and sparkly eyes still existed but his short-term memory had declined over that summer to the point that he had required several medical tests, psychology appointments, and a leave of absence from his thirty-eight-year government job. With Alzheimer's and dementia being officially ruled out – to our relief – his doctors were at a loss. In June, they threw him a diagnosis of "burnout" and washed their hands of him. (Nothing a few anti-depression and anti-anxiety pills could not fix, I guess.)

Only, they did not fix a thing. He did not need either of

them. He was neither depressed nor anxious. And yet, despite their magical all-fixing pill miscellany, he was not getting any better. He was declining rapidly in fact, and we all watched idly, hoping that the doctors were not wrong.

His behaviors had grown more peculiar and by the time the birthday party rolled around in late August we all silently feared that the problem was much worse than something that would only require some oral medication. When he reached forward from his chair to place his water cup onto my kitchen table, he missed the surface by nearly eighteen inches dropping the water glass to the cream-colored ceramic tile and soaking the floor and his feet. When he leaned forward while sitting on the couch to tie his running shoes, he lost his balance and went off-kilter, falling off the couch, and to his hands and knees. And then, he wet himself.

After months of running red lights and consequently revoking his own license from himself, forgetting where he put anything down merely thirty seconds earlier, walking around with misbuttoned shirts, never understanding what time of the day it was, the incontinence is what did it. My stepmother, Jackie, took him from the birthday party to the emergency department of our local hospital. From there he underwent several scans, and a massive brain tumor, causing severe swelling of the brain, was revealed. Surgery would happen within a few days.

In a flash, life went from cozy to terrifying. For days, my body shook, and my breath faltered. I dropped everything to be there for every second of the unknown and scariest first steps of what would no doubt be a long road to recovery. I paused the wife gig and the mother gig and the functioning gig and just tried to methodically breathe my way back to being a daughter.

Surgery happened on August 29. There were no words to describe the vile feeling as we waited and waited for thirteen hours in a shared family waiting room knowing that my dad's head was split wide open, the intact part of his face draped in a blue sterile sheet, with a strategic hole cut out for access as if he were a corpse – limp and cold and dead weight. A flap of skull sat idly on a table by the surgeon while he stared at and prodded my dad's exposed brain like a science project.

I wondered what it looked like – the skin flapped back over his face; the size of the chunk of ivory skull they had skillfully removed; the color of brain matter…. And then in as much time as it would take for that thought to appear, my stomach would go queasy, and I would nearly hurl.

At the end of that long day, a neurosurgical resident would call Jackie, me, and my brother, Richard, into the hallway for an update. Even though every nerve in our bodies jumped to life and our hearts beat like rapid fire at the sound of our names, we had to drag our heavy, tired, atrophied bodies from the uncomfortable leather chairs where we had left thirteen hours' worth of body indentations. You do not dare leave a waiting room while a surgery of that magnitude takes place. You do not risk missing one single thing going wrong or right.

With all our effort, we made our legs move us from the chairs to the hallway and got an update that things had gone pleasantly well. We asked what that would mean for longevity and expected an answer of fifteen to twenty years. (Why else cut someone's brain open and go through a procedure so seemingly barbaric if not for a good decade?)

"One year," he answered.

The three of us gasped in unison then froze. We were perfectly still other than the rapid fire of our hearts that had started up again. I could feel it reverberating through my body. I wondered for an instant if it was even my heart I was hearing or Jackie's, or Richard's. My face felt like fire. My stomach felt volcanic. None of us could look at each other. We waited until the resident wished us a good night and walked back down the hall. *Fuck him,* I thought. Then we collapsed into a pile of mixed limbs and tears and a lot of cries that I would not have recognized as any of our own voices. I am not sure, in that moment between the three of us, whose arms or legs or tears were whose. We were an entanglement of battered and broken hearts. One year.

He came home six days later. We had set up everything he needed to be cared for by Jackie (a former personal support worker) at their home and I had decided to only work part-time in order to be at their house two to three days a week to support or relieve Jackie. Since she had to become his full-time caregiver, I needed to become hers. With the full support of my husband, our family would go with a fraction of my already humble paycheck and figure out the rest later. I was not going to waste one single second of my dad's time here.

Three days after he came home from the hospital was my thirty-seventh birthday. I hated myself for thinking that it could be my last one with him. I wanted in every way to stay positive, but reality kept creeping back in. My wish was to share ice-cream cake with my dad – the simplest of wishes. Isn't it always the simplest of wishes when we look at what matters in life? So, an afternoon and evening back at my house with ice-cream cake is how we celebrated. And I knew that my birthday would never feel the same lightness and joy it always had, ever again.

As I waited for my mom to answer, my heart rate acceler-ated. I could not put my finger on why. Maybe it was noth-ing. I was being irrational. Naturally, after a diagnosis as earth-shattering and unexpected as my dad's, my head would probably go to irrational assumptions for a long time. I took in a slow breath through my nose and let it out to the count of three. I needed to calm myself down.

Her answer seemed normal.

"Hey, Kid," but there was a quiver in her voice. A break in her usual upbeat stride. It was subtle, but I caught it, and my breathing technique came undone. "What's wrong, Mom?"

"Well," she started, dragging out the short "e" to buy herself time to craft her next words delicately. "I don't want you to panic, but I had sort of a weird fainting thing yesterday. Marc got pretty scared and called the ambulance and I was taken to the hospital in Carleton Place and had a CT scan."

She made the details all sound so trivial. I could picture her eyes rolling and the submissive wave of her left hand as she spoke, as if referring to "all of this" – the emergency room, heart monitors, and loose-fitting faded blue gown imprinted with bubbles that tied up only at the back – was all just ridiculously unnecessary, as s if Marc, her husband of seventeen years, had overreacted.

"I am fine, okay, doll? But you are not going to believe this part, and this is where I do not want you to panic. They saw just two little spots on the CT scan of my brain and actually brought me to the Civic Hospital to be admitted to neurosurgery." The exact hospital, the exact unit, my dad had walked out of three days prior. "I am here now, waiting for an MRI and to see a neurosurgeon. I am in the exact place your dad was. Weird, eh?"

On the very day my dad was in surgery, my mom came straight to the hospital after work. She showed up to let me fall apart, settle my brother's knees when they bounced and support the woman that had now taken the title that she once occupied as my dad's wife. All that time, all that day, she had unknowingly sat there with two tumors in her head.

"Mom," I gasped, "What are these spots? How little are

they?" I asked her this, knowing that she did not have the answer and likely would not tell me yet if she did. Not yet. Not the morning after I had just spent my birthday with my dad, fearing it would be our last, desperately trying to freeze every possible glance his way as a still frame in my memory. She gave me the sort of passive answer I had come to expect from her after a precise thirty-seven years plus one day of life with her. "Just little, nothing to worry too much about."

I told her I would be there as soon as I could and she told me, of course, not to rush.

I hung up, standing erect and unwavering for what felt like forever. It could have been only thirty seconds. It could have been ten minutes. Time and matter had stopped in my new altered reality. My head spun with the rest of the world. My thoughts spiraled, and I knew that if I did not stop them, they would strengthen into a funnel cloud that would destroy every shred of hope in its path. I had to get control of myself. The spinning was throwing me off balance and I reached my hands out to grip the edge of my bed in an attempt to keep my entire body from collapsing to the ground. I stood there, in that supported bent over position until I could breathe in a full slow breath, then steadied myself upright to head downstairs to try to get myself back to the hospital, again.

The questions I asked myself on the ride back to the Civic Hospital that day are likely the same questions you are or have been asking yourself as well. *Can I get through this without having a mental breakdown? How am I going to be okay? Am I going to be okay? How the fuck am I going to do this?*

If you are in that same position, caregiving with fear of burning out, I have been there. You are not alone. The fear is real. You have been called upon as a caregiver. It is not a job we ask for but one we are assigned. And it is certainly a job that has us questioning whether we have the strength for it, every step of the way.

The cost of staying in this limbo of self-doubt and perpetual panic is going to wreak havoc on your mental and physical health. You may not have asked for this, but here it is, dropped into your lap. You are the only one now who gets to decide how you handle it, how you move forward with it. You can choose to do it with grace, grit, and a willingness to get uncomfortable and dig deep, or you can choose to do it with bitterness, resentment, angst, and a deteriorating sense of self and health. It is a choice. It is just not an easy process.

When you are watching someone whom you adore stare down the face of a terminal illness, you are also staring down the irrevocability of your world with them in it. Once you have accepted your situation for what it is, you have every heartbreaking but beautiful opportunity to love this person until the end. To show them true and unconditional love, to let them leave this world with dignity and not a shred of doubt of who they were, the legacy they will leave, the lives they have touched, and the hearts that they held. This incredibly profound opportunity has now become yours. And you can do it with your head high, your shoulders back, and with the strength to take care of *you* at the same time. This could be the single biggest honor of your lifetime.

The outcome may be inevitable. It is for all of us, truly. But how you get there and what you have left to hold onto afterward can be sculpted. The sharp edges of grief can be slightly chiselled and softened through your opportunity to take steps, one moment at a time, toward the goodbye too many people never get the chance to have. Take the time right now to dig deep inside yourself and decide if it is worth it to you to not just read the steps in this book but to truly put them into action, allowing yourself to be the best caregiver you can be. Help build a legacy for your loved one.

Remind them of the true meaning of loving without conditions. Show them there is dignity in transitioning to whatever magic awaits them on the other side, and make sure you are doing it all with the mindset to grow into exactly who you were meant to be.

2

SURVIVING THE UNIMAGINABLE

The ride to the hospital was interrupted with involuntary bursts of nervous laughter. The silence was too much, but the laughter caught me off guard. It felt foreign, like it was coming out of someone else's body. My cousin Jamie in the driver's seat, knowing full well that I was in no condition to operate a motor vehicle, and me slumped beside her: the two of us spontaneously breaking into fits of apprehensive giggles and then teetering back to impenetrable silence.

My purpose in sharing my story with you in such a vulnerable way is not to show you how unimaginably hard it has been but to show you how unimaginably far I have come. In recognizing yourself in my experience you will learn that you can survive this too. Every descriptive detail I write, every tear-inducing moment I share is meant to light the path through tragedy for you. You will find growth through this challenge in the same way that I did. I know that you will. Find yourself in my struggles and then look for yourself in my triumphs as you learn ways to create your own.

I carefully made my way back down the stairs after the

phone call with my mom and found Jamie in the playroom with the kids. She turned at the sound of my unsteady footsteps coming around the corner and with one quick look at me, dropped whatever toy was in her hand and walked straight toward me with an urgency that I understood to be her ability to read everything from the look on my face. "What happened?" she asked in a shaky voice. *Gerry*, she had thought. *Something has already happened to Uncle Gerry.*

She reached for me before she even finished the question and caught me as I collapsed into her. The words escaped me shaky and staccato, and much louder than I had meant for them to.

"My mo-om ha-a-a-s a brain tu-umor."

"What? No. What?"

Jamie held onto me long enough to ensure I was not going to fall on my face when she pulled away. Then she made a few quick calls to cancel the rest of her plans for the day, packed up our stuff, and got us loaded into the car to get to the hospital as quickly as we could. "This time," she stated as she looked directly into my eyes, hands gripping my shoulders, "I am not going to let you do this alone."

The drive up the spiral ramp of the hospital's tall parking tower was eerily familiar. The long walk down the stark main corridor was as unsettling as the first day I arrived there for my dad. I passed the gift shops with their plush slippers and cancer caps. *Would I be needing to stop in there soon? Would she lose all her hair? Were these "little spots" going to be brain cancer too?* Nothing would come into focus. I talked myself into putting one foot in front of the other until we made it to the double doors of the emergency department. I knew these doors well.

It was when I saw my mom that something changed in me. My mom was stoic. Her hair was always perfectly coiffed. Her nails were always painted. She was understated and classic in the most naturally beautiful way. A large gap in her front teeth gave her ear-to-ear smile and straight white teeth the perfect imperfection. It was her signature characteristic, coined "The Poirier Gap" after her maiden name and its strong presence through our family tree, including myself once upon a time before regretfully covering them up with porcelain veneers. I wish now that I had appreciated my gapped teeth's stellar beauty then. While she sat small in a hospital bed, wearing that faded blue, bubble-printed gown, loosely draped over her jeans, she flashed me that same smile, not an ounce of worry on her face. I was comforted momentarily – my mommy. And then just as quickly, my eyes left her and darted around the curtained-off section of the room. The monitors, the equipment, the tubes … none of them connected to her but all of them looming over us like a dark and threatening foreshadowing cloud. I had seen them all hooked up into my dad only days before.

"I'm fine, Kid, okay? Don't you worry about a thing." She said as I leaned over her for a hug. She squeezed me extra long and extra tight. I wondered how she was possibly remaining this calm. Then again, I am not sure that I would have recognized her any other way. Calm, cool and collected was exactly the way my mom always was. Nothing shook her.

But something in the most hidden part of my subconscious bubbled to the surface – a knowing that I wanted to unknow. I wanted to be as calm as my mom. I wanted to feel as secure in positivity as she appeared to feel. I wanted her unwavering faith that everything was in God's hands and that everything *was* going to be okay. But this nagging part of my brain was telling me something that my conscious thoughts would not yet accept or verbalize. This was not going to be okay.

I looked at her again – dollar-store bifocals now perched

low on her nose, red blackberry in hand as she typed away like a madwoman, thumbs rhythmically tapping the screen in fast forward speed, continuing with her workday as if nothing at all was going on. She had been working as a sales representative for Levelor Canada – a company that designed and made window blinds – for nearly seventeen years. She adored her job as much as her coworkers adored her. A mutual love affair. "Just have to email a store quickly to let them know that the mahogany faux woods have been discontinued." This is what she did, always acted like nothing was wrong, never wanting to burden anyone with the task of worrying about her. The knowing inside me returned, giving me a glimpse into the double caregiving journey I was about to embark on and sparking something in me, right then and there, that would have me searching deep inside myself for a newfound strength necessary to push through.

The thing about this "newfound strength" that you may be searching for is that it *already exists* inside of you. If you are wondering whether you can do this without losing your mind, I am here to tell you that you can. It will not be fun or easy and you will be down and out on many, many occasions, but the key here is to build resiliency so that when you are down you can get back up. We cannot strengthen as daughters, sons, spouses, siblings, and caregivers if we do not learn to give our lows the space they need, honor the feelings, and rise again.

I taught myself exactly this. It took more digging deeper than I ever thought I could. My dad, on the other hand, spent nearly ten years of my upbringing coaching my soccer teams. He used the "dig deep" term often, teaching us that whoever wants the win most the deepest. The win in this case may not apply to miracles (those are for prayers and God) but for ensuring that you are still standing, and even better, moving forward at the end.

You will see in this book that there were moments where I did not know how I would go on in a world without my parents. I especially had, and will share, moments where I did not think that I could go on through the pain that I was about to enter in watching them slip away. Using a combination of tools taught to me by my mom and dad, or lessons that I picked up as I went along, I put together an arsenal that I could pull from when needed. It did not come easily though, and I wonder if things would have been smoother for me if I had had a book like this one before facing each step. Would I have walked into the fire with the bravery of my dad? Would I have approached each obstacle with the stoicism of my mom? Instead, I gathered and grew as I went along. I went from scared and shaking to growing a non-profit organization to raise money for the caregivers of glioblastoma patients and establishing an online support group for caregivers of glioblastoma. Now, I work one-on-one with the people like me who are still sitting, scared and shaking and wondering if they have what it takes.

In between the moments now where I long for my parents, I am a more patient and compassionate mother and wife. I am the most devoted sister. I have little time or energy for things that sucked the life out of me before I became a caregiver. I have learned to protect my energy while still loving vulnerably. I am rewarded daily with support from around the globe and the immense satisfaction of living on purpose. I have become a caregiver coach, not unlike the way my dad coached me through sports and with many of the same approaches. My charity, the Slay Society, has raised over $60,000 in its first year of operation through hands-on fundraising initiatives and helped thousands of people around the world.

In sharing the most grueling and heart-wrenching moments, I will teach you to become who you were meant to be. I will teach you to laugh when the moment allows; breathe when things get hard; keep moving when you can; become an advocate; love them until the end; create a legacy for them; even help other people along the way. And the most miraculous part is that I am still standing. I was able to say goodbye to both my mom and my dad without a single regret and to let them go with nothing but love.

With this book, my coaching, and a willingness to explore hard places, you will too. They deserve that and so do you.

3

SLAY ONE DRAGON AT A TIME

No amount of blinking was making any of it believable. I squeezed my eyes closed, then popped them open, hoping that would shake the tricks in my head loose. But every time I opened them, I was seated at that round table, Jamie to my right, my dad to my left, Jackie next to him, then my mom, then her husband Marc, then back to Jamie. We were a ring of fragmented pieces trying desperately to hold ourselves together as a full family circle who had just been handed a double blow.

Once broken puzzle pieces trying to make themselves fit, and this time, not for the grandchildren. All we were missing was my brother, who was on his way, and my husband, who was at home with our children trying to dodge questions about why mommy was crying so hard and more likely, still just trying to keep himself upright from the shock.

It was Monday, September 9. It had been only two days since my birthday, the day that I sullenly ate ice-cream cake with my dad and blew out a handful of candles knowing full well that my wish for a miraculous recovery was probably going to be wasted. Two days since my mom had fallen victim to what turned out to be a seizure, caused by the tumors, in her kitchen across the city from my dad's and my ice-cream-cake-eating bond-fest.

She had fallen on Saturday in the late afternoon. She had texted me the following morning. It is important here to note that her husband, Marc, paced the emergency room that evening, cell phone in hand, saying, "I'm going to call Laura." My mom, however, always looking out for my best interest with one swift shake of her head said, "No, you sure are not. We are not calling my daughter on her birthday while she celebrates with her dad, knowing that it could be his last, to tell her that now I am here too."

Monday morning, my dad and Jackie came to the hospital. They were as shocked as any of us had been over the past sixteen days. I had arrived early in the morning, leaving Kenny to get our three kids up, fed, dressed, packed, and ready for school. Jamie met me there and my younger brother, Richard, was on route.

My dad and Jackie entered my mom's hospital room with their jaws on the floor. She had been moved from the emergency room up to the seventh-floor neurosurgery department early that morning. She was two rooms down from what had been my dad's. The walk through the hallways for them was also painfully familiar – uncomfortably comfortable. They managed to never burst into involuntary nervous laughter as I did though. They were much more composed.

As my dad paraded himself out of the elevator and made the sharp right turn into the neurosurgery unit, heads turned. It was not just the telling thirteen inches of scar held tightly together with forty-two staples and still bulging with red angry skin that caught people's eye, but the fact that he was back. Every nurse, nurse practitioner, doctor, custodian, and patient did a double take as he passed, flocking to him to ask him what had happened. What was the problem? Why was he back here? "It's not me this time." He would state in stunned shock. "It's my ex-wife."

When they entered the room, they split themselves between hugging me and hugging my mom. Then they switched. Then they hugged Marc and Jamie. It was one big hug-fest. The three other women in the shared room must have felt left out. I considered going and hugging each of them too. At least the ones that were not connected to too many drainage tubes that I could dislodge. I refrained.

The five of us stood around my mom in her bed. She was still dressed in her usual day clothes, hospital gown draped over top. She was still wearing sensible walking shoes for her all-day-on-your-feet sales job. She still thought she might get to one of her stores before her surgery. It had been scheduled for the next morning. At some point, the suggestion came up that we all head to the cafeteria for a snack and a change of scenery. For some of us, it had been two straight days of hospital room walls. For others, it had been sixteen.

We got a big round table in the middle of the cafeteria and dotted ourselves around it in no particular order. While my double-sided parent generation talked nonchalantly about how many calories were in a Sprite Zero, I tried the blinking myself back to reality thing. I noticed Marc across the table and registered how scared and uncomfortable, how shaken he seemed. He was a ball of nervous energy. He perpetually had one leg bouncing and was always adjusting the neck of his shirt, as if rooms were always too hot and shirt collars were always too tight for him. I wondered if my presence was making him any more anxious than the sheer fact that his wife was about to have her brain opened up. How could it be that we are back here, seated across from each other at the same table, no words spoken about our past? But then, it would take a cataclysmic event to have brought us back here. In my heart, there was no other way I could have forgiven him for what his years of alcohol abuse had done to my mom, to our family, unless there was a genuine apology from him, or a death in the family. I still was not sure which would come first.

I watched as my dad watched my mom, eyes full of love and remorse. Not remorse for a marriage failed – they had mutually come to that conclusion through years of their thoughts and behaviors – but remorse for her suffering. Remorse to see that this woman that he had once loved, still loved, the mother of his children, would be subject to the same kind of suffering that a brain surgery would bring. *Was it possible,* I could hear him wondering, *that she has the same diagnosis as I do?*

Suddenly Jackie rose from the table, grabbed her purse off the back of her chair, and meandered her way through the sea of scattered square and round cafeteria tables and toward the kitchen. She returned moments later with an armful of Sprite Zeroes. My attention shifted over to her now as she made her way around the table handing a drink to each – my dad, Marc, and then finally my mom.

This is where I broke. Jackie, my stepmom, taking care of my mom, the ex-wife. Two parents. Twin tumors. Another surgery. Another thirteen-hour waiting room day. But here we were, doing it together. Nothing made any fucking sense.

My heart filled and shattered all at once. The sudden sobs were explosive and uncontrollable. Sixteen days ago, I did not think I was going to survive the news of a brain tumor, surgery, recovery, and then six months of treatment with one parent. We had barely even begun that journey and now here I was again, facing the first three things on that list and potentially, another brain cancer diagnosis. How was I going to do this? I could not. How would I ever be expected to? Did people in my situation just die? Did they give up and take their lives, knowing that the heartache they were about to be slammed with seemed worse than the alternative? Or did they drop dead of spontaneous overwhelm? It was feeling more and more possible.

My heart was beating as fast as hummingbird wings, but as loud as a jack hammer. I could not slow it down. *I am having a heart attack*, I thought. *This is how it happens. This is how this sort of situation kills someone from shock. It's happening.* The sobbing wouldn't stop. I was dry heaving. I folded my arms onto the table and dropped my head into them. I had lost the strength to hold my head up on my own. The emotions surged within me and through me and out of me, leaving me tremoring from the aftershock.

The heaviest weight sat on my shoulders. How was I going to survive this? I was ashamed of myself in that moment. Here were my two parents beside and across from me, both newly diagnosed with brain tumors. One just finished and one facing a craniotomy. (Did I mention that my mom would be awake for hers?) Both possibly to be diagnosed with brain cancer. And here I was, with all my health and wellness and hockey-playing body, with three beautiful children at home and the most wonderful and hilarious husband, and the support of the whole world yet reduced to a puddle of tears making a loud sobbing scene in a hospital cafeteria while *they*, my mom and dad, the ones with the tumors in their heads, consoled me.

Jamie rubbed my back. I finally lifted my head, looked up at Marc through blurred, throbbing eyes and said, "I hated you. I hated you and now we are here. Now, I love you because we have to love each other to get through this." He looked at me with compassion, shame, bewilderment and through tears of his own said, "I love you too, Laura. And we will get through this, all together." Jackie echoed the same sentiment. My stepparents were now going to take care of my parents. Not only their spouses, but each other's.

My heart would not slow down, and my head would not stop spinning. I thought that what I was experiencing might be a nervous breakdown, right there in that moment. I wondered if my thoughts would spin so far that I would get up, lose all control, and do something volatile, violent, or scary. I felt as though my brain might snap, hurdling me into a terrifying mental state beyond return. I hyperventilated as my family watched on, unsure of what to do with me. I decided right then and there that I needed to walk myself up to the sixth floor and admit myself into the psychiatric ward.

I announced this to the table, and they all stared at me concernedly. "I'm serious you guys," I sobbed, "I don't know if I can do this. I think I am going to have a breakdown. I'm so scared." Each word heaving out of me with a matched force from the one before. "What do you think would happen? Do you think they would take me? Do you think they would let me stay and take care of me if I refused to leave until they did?" I had never been so terrified in my entire life. I did not want to face life anymore. Not like this. Not that I wanted to end it all, but I did not feel that I could face all that was coming and then turn around and go home, switching hats to my mommy one, cooking pasta, and patiently repeating reminders to empty lunch bags and put away back packs and choose healthy snack options. I didn't care about any of it now. If I went home, I would fail. Maybe if I went upstairs and begged to be admitted I would not have to. Surely the psych ward would hear my story and admit me into a room without hesitation.

"It doesn't work like that though, honey," Jackie said softly, breaking my train of unravelling thoughts. "You would have to go to the ER, and they would assess you and admit you from there. But they would most likely send you home. You are not a threat to yourself." I knew this. I knew that I was not a threat to myself in that moment but feared beyond measure that I could snap and become one. I considered hurting myself to get in. As if the psych ward had become some sort of vacation spot in my mind. I was desperate for an escape from all of this.

My parents divorced when I was seventeen and Richard was sixteen, shattering our worlds both temporarily and permanently. Any child of divorced parents knows that once the rubble is cleared, life and joy and love can be found and things move on in a different way, but nothing ever feels the same and you never stop longing for the foundational normal you once knew. Then, a handful of years later, they each remarried, providing us a new and uncomfortable normal that would take years of growth and therapy to fit into. We had fought tooth and nail, every single one of us, clawing our way back to a family unit that felt cohesive, familiar, palpable.

After seventeen years of Marc's exhausting struggles with alcohol abuse, my husband and I decided that to protect our family, and my nerves, we would need to shut him out from our lives until he became sober. I had not spoken to him in five years when my mom dropped to the ground in their kitchen on my birthday. My relationship with my mom never changed. We had always spoken daily. Her life goal was to retire and spend more time with her grandchildren. Teach them to sew. Teach them about Jesus. Soak in every moment, every laugh, every hug. A broken relationship between her husband and her daughter did not stop her from putting them at the center of her universe.

When my dad met Jackie online almost fifteen years ago, he quickly moved her into our home. The quick clash of our personalities created a heartbreaking aftermath and I quickly found myself without a home to live in. I had gone to live with my elderly grandmother until I could save enough money for my place and a car. The relationship between my dad and me was momentarily severed. But with a lot of tears and work and vulnerability, we worked our way back to a healthy relationship. It seems now a blip in time. But a blip that caused more damage to me than most other trials in my life.

And now, there we all were – me, two parents, two step-parents, three tumors – all sitting around a big fat table in a big, fat cafeteria with a big, fat new reality dumped on top of us twice. Would we be forced to put all past differences aside and get through this together? Was there any other option? Could I do this? I had to do this. How was I fucking going to do this?

And here is the answer: love.

It got clear quickly that the only way I was going to be able to take care of two dying parents and not fall apart was with pure love – love for them, love for my stepparents, and love for myself.

SHARPENING YOUR SWORD

Over the next few chapters, I will break down that love into eight manageable steps that you will be able to apply to your already grueling day-to-day routine without feeling extra overwhelmed. Together, we will get you to a place of calm, peace, and confidence in your caregiving that will result in a deepened sense of self.

My dad had a motto in life – slay one dragon at a time.

When I was a headstrong teenager overwhelmed with compiling school assignments, this is what he would tell me.

Oddly enough, this is the saying he offered to my mom, over and over, after her diagnosis was delivered too. He used this to calm us, to teach us not to bite off more than we could chew, and to show us that if we could stop looking at the big picture and break things down into smaller manageable steps, anything was accomplishable. In order to slay a dragon, you will need to sharpen your sword with manage-able tools and steps.

For him, step one was a craniotomy. He worried about step two only after step one.

Stick with me as I help you navigate your way through, slaying one dragon at a time.

You are going to learn how to breathe your way through panic attacks and better yet effectively avoid them in the first place.

You are going to learn to play the part and how to settle into the role of being a caregiver.

You are going to get organized so that you can best manage the never-ending schedule of appointments and medications.

You will learn to create the type of environment you will need for yourself as a caregiver to heal and grow without distractions and negativity from the outside world.

You will work toward losing the fear of the disease itself and the unknowns it may carry by educating yourself to build confidence in your ability to provide the care, medical needs, and advocacy your loved one needs.

You will stifle through the myth that is self-care and create a list of realistic ways you can practice self-love and raise your frequency. (Pst, you're doing it already.)

You are going to dig deep into the hardest and most uncomfortable feelings and learn to embrace and work through them with your head high and shoulders back instead of hiding from or burying them. There, and only there, is where you will strengthen your arsenal to be able to love them to the end without unravelling.

Lastly, you will be inspired to use the fuel of your antici-patory grief, grief, or anger, as a fire starter for change around not only your life but lives of others who are fighting or caregiving around the same disease. You will be motivated to use your platform for betterment and will have built resiliency to rise back up each time that you are down, no matter how long it takes. You have been given a glimpse into this world so that you can change it.

On second thought, maybe lastly is not the right way to start that last paragraph because while that is what the steps are all about, the biggest thing you are going to get form this book is your beautiful metamorphosis into the richest, fullest, most love-filled version of yourself.

Let's start slaying dragons.

4

INHALE. EXHALE

After my award-winning public breakdown in the hospital cafeteria, my dad and Jackie left for his first meeting with his oncologist. Long before my mom's diagnosis (which is realistically a time frame of under ten days), I had planned to attend this appointment with them and so I collected myself from the cafeteria table and joined them. I left my mom in the hospital with Jamie, Marc, and her brain tumors in order to go hear from the next doctor what the plan of attack would be to fight my dad's cancer.

The thing about glioblastoma, which you may have already gathered by now, is that the prognosis is grim. In a textbook case doctors will dish out a life expectancy of twelve to eighteen months, give or take. That is what the surgical resident had told Rich, Jackie, and me on the night of my dad's craniotomy, catching us off guard and knocking us to our knees. The only person they had not told, however, was my dad. For nearly two weeks the rest of us walked on eggshells – very, very thin eggshells – and bit through our tongues when he would ramble on about getting out of the hospital, recovering, and heading back to university after his six-month chemo treatment ended to obtain a master's degree in Indigenous Women's Studies. It was excruciating knowing what he did not know.

What we were told by the surgeons was that the oncologist would gently tell him the news at his first appointment. How I wish we had not known first. How I wish we had not had to stare him in the eye and force a smile and nod every time his eyes brightened as he spoke of the future when we had been informed that all we may have is the right now. I hated that part. It felt like lies and deceit. None of it was fair.

There we were, on our way to the appointment where a complete stranger would look my dad straight in the eye and tell him that as per his prediction, and histories, he may only live about one year – not long enough to obtain a master's.

Watching them fill out the paperwork in the waiting room of that appointment was gut-wrenching enough. Knowing what was coming next was far worse. With every passing "tick" of the clock on the wall above us, my stomach tightened more.

Finally, we were called into an exam room by a well-built, middle-aged nurse with straight chin-length hair and were given a row of four single plastic chairs against the wall to cozy ourselves into. Jackie led my dad into the room with a guiding hand on his arm as he reached out and touched every possible wall or doorway for support. I clamored in behind them holding all purses, jackets, and clipboards with health history forms.

The nurse took vitals and asked a gazillion questions which my dad did his best to answer, but Jackie mainly corrected for him. I chimed in with the odd clarification on date and timeline details – my gift of a photographic memory – but otherwise missed most of what they were saying because the anticipation of the prognosis delivery was too much for me to handle. I was too focused on slowing my heart rate down to hear much else.

Then it happened. The oncologist entered – tall, slim, middle-aged, soft grey hair with alabaster skin and about the most pleasant and gentle demeanor you would ever see. He had not even spoken a word, yet we already knew the words would come softy. And they did.

Dr. Nicholas shook our hands, offered his sympathies for a tough situation, and proceeded to draw us diagrams on his clipboard that gave the best representation of what was going on inside my dad's head that we had seen so far. He explained radiation and chemotherapy in a way that made the treatment world far less terrifying. He had done this before.

I was mesmerized by him, by his embodiment of the word "gentle." I wanted to give him a hug. I wanted to ask if he could come stay with us a while and maybe by just being there everything would feel calmer. I had almost entirely forgotten that I had a mother in a hospital twelve minutes away or that a conversation about life expectancy was about to knock me off my chair until he smiled, nodded, slowly turned his clipboard over in his lap – closing that chapter of the meeting – and addressed my dad again.

"Has anyone talked to you about life expectancy?"

There it was. My heart rate accelerated like a Maserati on an empty four-lane highway under a full moon. But I didn't feel like the driver, I was in the passenger seat and there was no driver. I had no control. I thought I might cry, or puke, or die. All of my chest hurt, breathing hurt. I did not know what to do with my hands, my body, my face.

"Nooo," my dad answered with a drawn-out hint of hesitation. The conversation went on not in such a manner of, *well here it is, sucks eh?* but more of a patient-fueled question-and-answer period about whether or not he wanted to know and how much he wanted to know and how the number he was about to hear was only an average and how there are many people who live far *past* that prognosis – and many who don't.

I heard none of the rest of the words that came out of anyone's mouths but instead just sat there – shaking, leaning my elbows on my bouncing knees, and resting my head in my hands, cocked at such an angle that I could study my dad's face and pinpoint the exact moment where his heart would crack in half. Or maybe it would be mine.

Then it happened. There was a sudden widening of his eyes and a sharp breath. That was it. The moment. I looked away. I could not lift my eyes from the floor but could listen.

"Wow."

A pause.

"Okay. Well, that's not what I was expecting to hear at all." His words were interrupted with long inhales.

The rest of the appointment was a blur.

When we stood to leave and shake Dr. Nicholas's slender, warm hands again, he asked if there was anything else he could do for us. I looked up at him and said, "Yes, please. Could you also take my mom?"

As a young asthmatic hockey-, soccer-, and track-obsessed athlete, I grew up having multiple sports-induced asthma attacks per week. Too stubborn to ever get off the field or the ice or leave a game entirely, I would sit on the sidelines determined to breathe my way through the attack with as much focus as I had utilized in the game. It worked (almost) every time. (And it tested my parents' nerves on more than one occasion.)

The technique I used was this: breathe in through your nose for a count of three, hold it for two seconds, and breathe out through your mouth for a count of four.

Exhaling too quickly will allow less air into your lungs

and cause you to become nauseous and vomit – which many women do in labor, including me. Gross. The exhale must be as controlled as the inhale, both slow and intentional.

When you feel a moment of panic or lack of control start to come on, try this breathing technique. It is best if you can sit somewhere quiet. Excuse yourself from the hospital room if you can, head to the bathroom, get to the hallway. In moments where I could not leave, I would turn around and do this as I faced the window or pretended to be doing something on my phone.

There were moments where I would outright admit that I was breathing away the panic and there were moments where the mood in the room was too light and I did not want to bring it down with my fears so pretended to be tending to something else that faced away from my parents.

In that moment, we left Dr. Nicholas behind us and headed back through the heavy glass doors. I worked on my breaths while my dad worked on processing the fact that life as he had dreamed may never happen.

Jackie and my dad headed back home after the appointment for some much-needed rest. As a recovering brain surgery patient, he could not get away with much movement or thinking without needing a nap and he undoubtedly had some thinking to do. I headed straight back to the Civic hospital where my mom, Marc, and Jamie had returned up to her hospital room, the one that sat two doors down from where my dad had been days earlier. My mom looked small again in the stark white hospital bed.

We had yet to meet the neurosurgeon. We had gotten MRI results as read by the nurse practitioner. We knew now that the "spots" on the scans, as my mom had so dismissively referred to them, were, in fact, not just blips but actual tumors. However, we would not know the confirmed pathology until after surgery, where they would biopsy a piece of the tumor.

We had met a pile of nurses, the anesthetist, occupational therapist, physical therapist, registration employees, custodians, and she did not know it yet, but even her oncologist. We met everyone, it seemed, except for the neurosurgeon. That was the next dreaded visit. The big-time factor that would turn all of this from surreal to very, very real. If he did not exist, if he didn't walk in, then there was no confirming that any of this was happening. There was still a teensy sliver of hope that this was all a mistake, a misdiagnosed fainting spell caused likely by dehydration. That laughing possibility still existed somewhere out there and I was holding on tight to it.

At 6:30 that evening, he appeared in her room. He was as good looking as everyone said he would be. He was not the same surgeon my father had. He oozed with blue eyes and boy-like charm and dimples that expanded when he smiled. He could freeze you in your tracks. Something about the way he spoke made everything less scary too. But even with his calm, crooning voice, he still spoke the words that we did not want to hear.

"We can't know for sure until pathology results come back after surgery, but it does look like glioblastoma."

My tight grip on that slim possibility of a laughable misdiagnosis slipped through my fingers like a fistful of sand. Each falling grain tickling the skin of my palms with its reminder that this was happening all over again.

He assured us that there was a particularly good chance that it could still have been an astrocytoma. In the world of brain tumors (a world that I cannot quite accept needs to exist at all) there is a grading system, the same way that we rank other cancers in stages. A stage four cancer is usually considered terminal. A grade four tumor is also considered terminal. (Please note here that there are more and more people every day challenging the word "terminal" and living far past the number the doctors throw at them upon diagnosis.)

Dr. Sinclair, our well-known surgeon with the heart-melting smile, looked at me, perched up there on the windowsill, and said, "I'm sorry. I heard about your dad as well. I cannot imagine what this is like or how you are feeling. We will take good care of her, okay?"

He was right. He could not have known how I was feeling. No one could. Not unless you have unexpectedly been told that your seemingly healthy parent was dying and then told two weeks later that your other seemingly healthy parent was probably also dying of exactly the same thing. I did not even know how I was feeling. But I did know that my heart was beating so fast that it was all I could hear in my ears. I wondered, for the tenth time in that week, if it would either just stop suddenly or combust. My ears were throbbing with pulses of ringing sounds. I could feel the room spinning around me. Then suddenly, as Dr. Sinclair spoke, my entire body heated up and went flush. A wave of heat prickled my cheeks.

The throbbing, the spinning, the pounding heart – none of them were stopping. I was acutely aware that everyone was watching me, and I realized I had stopped breathing. It is surprising how something that we think should come so naturally can be completely forgotten by our subconscious when we are in a state of trauma. The trauma was telling my body that I would not survive this, and that all energy needed to be conserved. So by its own volition, my body stopped inhaling. I was sure that I was going to fall right off that ledge and smash face-first into the floor, unconscious, like my cherub-cheeked daughter had one day in the kitchen eight years earlier. I didn't dare move a muscle.

Just shy of my oldest daughter Leightyn's first birthday

she did just this. I had put her down on our kitchen floor while I chopped veggies for dinner. She wanted me to hold her so badly that she started screaming and crying. She was sitting there on her chubby diapered bum, crocodile tears streaming out of her big brown eyes, staring up at me as if the entire kitchen would swallow her whole in that moment if I did not pick her up. I turned back to chop a red pepper, offered her an empathic word of support like, "It's okay, Leightyn. You're fine," in my softest mommy voice, and then heard a thud. I turned at the noise and to my horror, my tiny, barely toddling girl was flat on her face and not moving. Her face was pressed straight into the floor, arms flailed out to her sides and legs still folded awkwardly underneath her. She did not budge.

I first just stared at her in disbelief, which disappoints me now, truthfully. I question why I had not moved to her faster. Why did I freeze in that moment? It was as if my brain was trying to process what I was seeing in slow motion before it could act on anything. It was an experience so unnatural that my mind had no idea how to take it all in and what to do with it. I sadly learned that day that when it comes to the well-known flight-fight-freeze response, I am a freezer.

I finally moved, picked up my limp baby, and proceeded to react by doing all the completely irrational and uncalm things that I probably should not have done. I screamed, I panicked, I fell apart. I thought she was gone.

Finally, after what felt like twelve minutes but was more realistically eight seconds, she came to. I called 911 panicked that she may have just experienced a seizure. They came right away, assessed her, deemed her to be stable, took her to the hospital as a precaution, and after a long six-hour stay into the wee hours of the night, we were told that she had simply held her breath and fainted. Who knew? A breath-holding spell is a real thing that kids do. The fainting is their body's version of self-defence. It says, *if you are not going to allow me any more oxygen then I am going to have to shut you down so that you are forced to naturally breathe again.*

She went on to pull six more of those episodes in that year but grew out of them by the time she turned two. Imagine your toddler, eyes rolling back into her head, face turning purple as air and life seemed to slip out of her body: it never got easier to watch.

Therefore, practicing breathing techniques is essential for controlling our body's reactions.

My feet, which had been drumming against the built-in radiator behind my heels from the moment the doctor had walked in, stopped suddenly, like pendulums that had lost their momentum. I pictured the pendulum that spent its life sitting on top of our piano in its dark walnut casing, throughout all my childhood. The piano that my dad had saved for and bought himself the year before I was born. It was his first baby. I was his second. His father had been a professional and wildly talented pianist and while my dad's life dreams steered more in the direction of number crunching and a solid Monday-to-Friday, nine-to-five, government job with a reliable paycheck, his dream home always included a piano that he could continue to pound away on, where he could teach his future children to play, and then his future grandchildren. The tinkling of piano keys and runs of chords and instrumentals of The Beatles make up the soundtrack of most of my life with him.

And today it would seem that along with that swaying pendulum, which had lost its momentum years before, both my mom and dad's lives would now start slowing down until they stopped.

In the case of me sitting on that window ledge, my body having stopped taking in oxygen while everything spun and whipped around me, my system was about to hit self-defence mode and shut me down when I caught it early enough to gasp in a breath of stale hospital air. That was enough to slow everything back down. It was enough for me to finally be able to latch onto some of Dr. Sinclair's words which seemed to be whirling around the room and to start piecing together what he had said. But I hated all of it.

"Surgery will be first thing in the morning," he said.

He left the room, leaving us all stuck to the same body positions we had held for the entire duration of his visit. All four of us were unable to move. All four of us were paralyzed by the unknowns. Not one of us was willing to admit it.

My mom, of course, spoke first. "You okay, Kid?" I could not look at her. I was still walking myself through the simple tasks of – inhale, exhale, inhale, exhale – with so much intention that if I stopped with the focused reminders, I would surely drop dead.

Jamie reached up and touched my knee. Her warm hand was comforting. I looked at her and exhaled again without breaking eye contact. She whipped her eyes over to the hospital room door and without words asked me if I wanted to get out of the room and get some air. I needed a change of scenery. I needed to breathe air that had not been circulated through the people in that stuffy room. Mostly, I needed to be able to break down in a place that was not directly in front of my stoic and apparently mortal mom. I finally had the strength to look at her as I slowly lowered my weak and tingly legs to the floor. My eyes caught hers and then welled up with tears. I forced another deep breath in through my nose while she tried to assure me that she was not going anywhere and promised me again that everything was going to be okay.

Jamie and I walked into the hall and collapsed side by side on the nearest bench. Neither of us spoke. My dad. Her uncle. My mom. Her aunt. What was there to say really? She asked me if I wanted her to start emailing the family (we have a French-Canadian Catholic family which basically translates to huge) to update them on tomorrow's surgery, and I used most of my energy just to nod yes.

While Jamie tapped away on her phone, I practiced breathing over and again over. I use the word "practiced" because even though breathing was intuitively supposed to happen without thought or force, I recognized that in my freeze mode only my conscious mind could control it. Without intentional steady breaths I would not be able to gain that same level of calm, leadership, or sanity, that I had just witnessed two exquisite doctors nurture while they delivered life-altering news to patients and families. I knew that for me to step into the role of caring for the two people who had always cared for me, the simplest thing I could do for them was control my breathing in order to control my thoughts when things felt like they were spinning out in the wrong direction. If this was hard, things were about to get a whole lot harder.

The best thing I learned though was to start these breathing techniques each morning when I got in my car to head to the hospital. I'd take ten deep breaths, then again before I got out of my car when there was time. I would also focus on my breathing as I walked down the hall and prepared to enter their rooms. Doing this as a preventative measure helped lower the number of panic attacks I had been experiencing each day.

Panic attacks can come on in so many different forms. Many people can sweat, feel dizzy, or nauseous. For many, there can be a sudden urge to cry that may seem completely unwarranted and certainly inconvenient. For me, the most common way panic would show up was in my heartbeat. I would experience sudden heart palpitations and most often they would come while I was driving my car or lying in bed trying to sleep.

This is quite common because, as a caregiver, your body and mind go into constant fight mode and stay there while you are caring for your loved one. Once you remove yourself from that scene and have a quiet place (like alone in your car or in your bedroom) to process what you have seen and experienced that day your body is finally able to manifest all that trauma and fear physically.

Take the time to focus on your breathing at different intervals throughout the day, even before you put your feet on the floor. Lie in bed when you wake up in the morning and practice this. Close your eyes and try for ten slow, steady, deep breaths before you get up. Use the three-two-four counting that I mentioned above. It does not have to be perfect. You will likely get interrupted by your thoughts and that is okay. If you do, gently guide yourself back to your breathing and continue counting from where you left off.

There is a fascinating docuseries on Netflix called *Lennox Hill* where Manhattan's power team of neurosurgeons, Dr. John Boockvar and Dr. David Langer, lead their surgical team in what they call a "mindful moment" before every surgical procedure. They take a minute to check in with themselves and with their staff, from residents to anesthetists to support nurses, ensuring everyone is breathing, calm, and centered. Wouldn't that make you feel good as a patient to know that your care team was grounded? Well, guess what, you are a part of your loved one's care team.

The moments of fear and panic are going to come up for you on this journey and are likely going to happen when you are not even doing anything scary or hard. Learning to master a few simple breathing techniques that you can pull out of your toolbelt will help you manage these moments when they happen unexpectedly. Learning to take a mindful moment before starting your day, and again during, will help cut these panic attacks down altogether and give you the guided focus you are going to need to keep being the best caregiver you can be.

The only way you can get there is to take care of yourself. Breathe love into yourself.

5

PLAY THE PART

The days dragged on after the night we met mom's neurosurgeon. Her first surgery was scheduled for that next morning and I made it back to the hospital by 7:00 a.m. along with Richard, Jamie, and Marc. It was September 10. I was thirty-seven years and three days old. We watched her get wheeled off – her turn to have her head cut open – and we made our way back to the family lounge waiting area that we had become so familiar with two weeks earlier.

The day was a blur, but I remember that we spent thirteen grueling hours – the same as we had with dad – sitting, standing, pacing, waiting. The chairs grew increasingly more uncomfortable by the hour, and I watched my tall, gangly brother awkwardly splay his body across several of them in a desperate attempt to get some rest.

We lived on coffee. Whenever a new family member or friend would arrive to accompany us for a stint in the waiting room, they would offer to bring anything we needed, and we would all request coffee. We would have hooked ourselves to a caffeine intravenous line if the option had been available. There were not many options for anything healthy within the hospital so typically those coffees would come accompanied with a box of donuts, muffins, or some other equally calorically dense but nutritionally void pastry.

Our bodies were fueled by garbage. We were not sleeping. I had not slept in two and a half weeks at that point. Between 2 sick parents, three school aged children and a busy landscaping business that I was still doing my best to be involved in, I was a zombie. I was a zombie who was trying to step into the role of wife, mother, daughter, business owner, and now trauma-wielding caregiver on nothing but caffeine and sugar, teetering on stable. It was a recipe for disaster.

Dr. Sinclair finally appeared at the entrance to the family lounge. He was head to toe in navy blue scrubs and cap. He looked only slightly more alert than we did. We had been surrounded by upwards of fifteen family members at any given time that day. We were, again, a revolving door of scared and worried people who shared a gene pool. By then though, it was just the core of us remaining. Richard, Marc, and I stepped into the hall to hear his update. He informed us that surgery had gone well and all of the larger tumor had been removed. He said that the second tumor would likely be removed in two days with another surgical procedure if she continued to recover well.

"Any questions?" he asked, likely hoping we would say no and end his long day in the operating room, allowing him to get home to his family. Then Richard asked the question that not a single one of us, nor the cyclical group of thirty family or friends who had rotated through that room with us over the past two and a half weeks had dared to question out loud, including me or Richard.

"Yes," my brother stated, "Should we be getting MRIs?" He waved a hand in my direction to show that the "we" meant me and him. My heart stopped. *Please God, let him snort a dismissive laugh so that we know that we have nothing to worry about. Please let the fear lingering in my mind over these past few days be for nothing.*

Sinclair looked down at his feet, shuffled his weight from his right leg to his left, and then looked back up at us. He let out a breath, looked straight from Richard to me, and back again, and with a defeated sigh said, "I would." I officially had one more layer of hell to add to the mix. My brother and I could have glioblastomas too. The doctors had never seen anything like this before. Was this disease going to take down our entire family? To date, there were no known genetic causes and no known environmental causes for glioblastoma. But that did not mean that there were no environmental factors, only that they had yet to be discovered. I would have to do what I had been avoiding doing so far: have this conversation with my husband, whom I knew had already been walking around cloaked with fear for my health since day one of my dad's diagnosis.

I spent every day at the hospital after that. After my dad's days in the hospital, I had been gifted a three-day break. That was it. That was all I would have again for a long time. I had three days from when he left the hospital – automatic doors closing with a whisper behind us, us waving goodbye to the historical red brick building with no intention of ever looking back – until my mom walked in.

September 12 would bring another long day. It had been only two days since my mom's first surgery and we would shuffle ourselves again back up to the third floor, make our way to the family waiting lounge and wait for the surgeon to come out again that evening in his navy-blue scrubs for another update. I wondered how many pairs of those he owned. Or if he ever chose a different color. We were well-practiced in this game by then. He broke it to us that after that second surgery, he did in fact think that these tumors

were both grade four glioblastomas but that still only
pathology results would confirm in a week or so. He
confirmed them to be malignant. Hope for a misdiagnosis
was fading.

The next day my dad had woken up with a clarity that he
had not been able to find for months since his cognitive
decline began. He had brain cancer. His ex-wife had brain
cancer. They were diagnosed fourteen days apart. Their
tumors were the same size and both in the right temporal
lobes. Something was not adding up. This was not a coincidence. He had been wracking his healing brain since the
morning after my birthday when he received a blubbering,
incoherent phone call from me, telling him that mom was
now in the hospital too. But then it hit him – an epiphany:
our old house. For whatever reason, call it luck or divine
intervention, he concluded that the link had to be our old
house.

My parents were typically complacently happy in their
marriage. We never saw them fight. They did not even so
much as disagree on dinner in front of us. I was the ardous
age of seventeen when they announced a divorce. Rich and I
were floored, confused, and oh so angry. They shared a
mutual love and respect for each other but lacked all the rest
of what a marriage should be. They had become roommates,
as so many couples navigating nearly twenty years of
marriage and parenting often do. They had not lost themselves in each other. They had lost themselves, period.

Their coping mechanism in this lonely reality was to
chase happiness, not choose happiness. We moved more
than most military families. The reasons varied: a bigger
house; a big custom-built house in the country; back to the
city because the country was too far; a smaller house to
save money…. The excitement of each change softened the
sting of their passion-void union for only a little bit until it

all came to the surface again and a new "for sale" sign went up.

When my dad shot out of bed that morning with an intuitive knowing that the link lied in our big country house – the one that my parents had built themselves with the help of my uncles when I was eight years old – he determinately told Jackie that they would have to drive out there that morning and talk to the people who lived there and all the neighbors. She shook her head at his unexpected persistence but he would not take no for an answer and so she obliged.

Later that afternoon he came barreling into my mom's hospital room blurting out, "Chris, we know what it is." We all stared at him. He had, after all, just had his brain messed with and was often making extraordinarily little sense.

"It was Burnt Lands Road. Jackie and I went back to the old house today and the woman living in our house has a brain tumor."

We all stopped to process. This could not be real.

"And the next-door neighbor died of a glioblastoma. We went to six houses and out of the six houses, four of them had cancer."

In the moment my dad lacked the ability to keep any insight as to how this new finding would affect my brother or me. While he was bursting with discovery, like Sherlock Holmes cracking a case, I was shaking inside. Richard and I had lived in that house too.

My dad spent every day after that using his connections in the city to reach out to members of parliament and government employees to help him look further into the cause.

The other person whom my dad had overlooked with his blunt news delivery was my husband. He was already anticipating my MRI with an overwhelming amount of fear and dread. Now he had concrete evidence to layer onto his parfait of theories that I would be next. This information was enough for Kenny to suffer a mental breakdown. For an entire week, he barely left our bed due to stomach-flu-like symptoms. We thought he was sick, so he stayed home from work. He even went to see our family doctor, who could not quite find anything symptomatic to diagnose him with. It was four days into this that I realized he was not sick at all. He had broken down. The fear, the overwhelm of trying to manage the kids on his own, the busy work season, the picking me up off the floor fourteen times a day, and now swallowing the blistering acceptance that these cancers could have been caused by the house his wife had grown up in … it had all become too much for him and his body had shut off.

My last supporting pillar had fallen, and I was left to manage everyone and everything by myself. I was losing complete control and grasping at anything that I could still hold onto. I was barely hanging on. My headaches had become so unbearable and were all presenting just behind my right temple, exactly where both of my parents' primary tumors were located. The pain would pulsate and stab into my temple with such intensity that I would stop dead in my tracks and hold the wall or a table to not collapse. I was certain that there was a tumor there, that I was next, and I feared for my brother's life as well. But I could not stop to think about it. I could not let my thoughts wander there yet. There were way too many other people, my husband now included, who needed me to lift them back up.

Social media post from September 14, 2019:

"Our rock has officially crumbled. Some superheroes wear colorful capes. Ours observes quietly from the sidelines, silently cheers us on, lifts us with strong arms when we fall, and works harder than anyone that I know to keep us in a life where mine can be the first face my children see after a long day at school. He is selfless. Asks for nothing and gives everything. But now, Kenny is broken. He is lost, terrified, and defeated. He has barely eaten or moved in five days. We are going to do our best to take care of him, but he needs all the love and support you can all possibly give him as he had stepped up to support his family through this nightmare, but it all became too heavy today. We are not sure how to put the broken pieces of this family back together and we are shaking with fear. Please continue rallying."

The morning after discovering Kenny's breakdown, I stood at my kitchen counter staring unblinkingly at my coffee pot percolating my morning cup of strength with tauntingly slow speed. It was 6:42 a.m. The kids were up and stirring in front of their morning television, our daily ritual before getting ourselves moving for the day. It had been a while since I had been home for this but today, I opted to get to the hospital a bit later and be home in the morning to take the morning responsibilities off Kenny. For some reason in that moment, I felt inclined to get a glass of water. I zombie-walked to the fridge, poured some water, and proceeded to chug the entire glass without realizing it. I instantly felt lifted. I felt hydrated. I felt elevated in a way that my body had not in a while, and in a way that coffee was not giving me. I poured a second glass and chugged it back too. It was as if my body was thanking me for finally listening to its pleas and giving it what it so desperately needed.

In that moment in the kitchen, it hit me that there was one thing I *could* control. I could drink water. It was the simplest thing. So simple that it seemed ludicrous to have been so enlightened and excited by this new revelation. But there it was. I could control the amount of water I put in my body.

I could not control the tumors, their fate, even my fate or dreaded risk of a tumor, but I could, without excuse, make sure I hydrated my body and maybe for right now, that was the only thing I could do. But it was manageable. I vowed that morning to make sure I started every single morning off with a large glass of water and to pack a water bottle for the day. It did not have to mean no coffee, but it had to mean stop making trauma an excuse for why I was treating my body so poorly. How was I going to take care of these two people (not to mention my three children, Kenny, and our dog, or *myself*) if I could not even do something as simple and necessary as drink enough water.

When you start a new job, any job, you play and dress the part. You are expected to show up with a certain demeanor, a trained skillset, or at the least, a growth mindset and willingness to learn. You get excited for a new job. You even buy yourself a new wardrobe so that you can look the way you think you need to look. You start out with a bounce in your step and a motivation to pack beautiful, colorful lunches, or meal plan, or shower more often. You do your hair a certain way and clean yourself up and present your beautiful confident self in a way the job calls for. Well, caregiving is no different. In fact, your parent has already been surrounded by caregivers in the way of nurses, doctors, and support staff that are doing just that every day for them.

While I know that caregiving for a dying parent is not a new job that you have eagerly signed up for, why can't you treat it the same way when it comes to how you show up for your loved one? They deserve the best of you. *You* deserve the best of you. Here is one easy way you can step into that role and keep yourself from falling apart.

HYDRATE

Let me tell you that this is going to be one of the most important things you will do for yourself for so many different reasons. Here are just a few.

Your body is made up of 60 percent water. Fill it back up.

Your brain alone is made up of 73 percent water. (That is why we get headaches when we are dehydrated.)

It may be a small task that you can control but it will remind your psyche that you still have more control over your life than you think you do.

It is the catalyst for so many other good habits. If you can start by making toting along a water bottle a habit, then you can move to packing a few healthy snacks a habit. Find time to meditate or be still in your day. Practice gratitude. Exercise. The good habit train is just getting going.

Water raises your frequency. We are all energy. When we raise the frequency of our energy (which yes, you get to control) then we attract higher energy around us and therefore can attract and manifest more good things and good health for ourselves, and for the parent we are caring for.

Here is a good rule of thumb for determining how much water you need. Take your body weight in pounds, cut it in half, drink that in ounces. Example: I am 160 pounds therefore I need approximately eighty ounces of water per day. That would be five to six tall glasses of water.

In North America, we are walking around as a chronically dehydrated population. Let's change that.

Every day became the same routine for me. Wake up. Breathe in. Breathe out. Repeat. Put feet on the floor. Head up. Shoulders back. Walk forward. (To the fridge first for water, as we have now established.) Those first minutes of my morning were the only ones I felt I had any control of. Any minutes that followed, between kids and hospital surprises, were a rollercoaster whose rickety cart I had been drugged, dragged, and stuffed into against my will. Except for the kids. Technically I totally signed myself up for that ride.

Some days I would head to the hospital first thing in the

morning, leaving Kenny to get our three confused kids ready and off to school on his own. Other days I would stay home in the morning to get them to school myself (some feeble attempt at the old normal) and then head straight to the hospital. But each morning was so rushed and hectic and my head was never there, at home, with my children. My head was always at the Civic, in those historic red brick walls, on that dreaded seventh floor.

I would get my coffee at home in the morning, then another when I arrived at the hospital from the Tim Horton's in the main lobby as I picked up one for my mom or my dad, whichever parent was in the hospital at the time (sometimes both). When a visitor arrived later in the day, they would come armed with a round of coffee and treats again. My mind, already a mess from the reality that I was trying to process with my parents, my mortality, and the lack of sleep, was continuously foggier and foggier due to my improper feeding and nutrition. I was becoming even less able to cope with news or day-to-day tasks without breaking down than I had already been.

It hit me again one morning as I lay in bed, breathing, and preparing to put my feet on the floor, that I still could be a better caregiver than I was being. If I was going to put myself in a position to be caregiving full-time, added to my full-time mom-ing and wife-ing and business owner gigs, then I needed to play the part even more so than just drinking enough water. The decision had been made that my mom would come and live with me and my family once she was discharged from the hospital.

Dr. Nicholas, the oncologist, had quickly agreed to take on my mom as a patient. In his decades of experience being the only glioblastoma oncologist in Ottawa, this was something he had certainly never seen before. We had set both of my parents up with the same radiation oncologist, Dr. Nair, as well. They would start daily radiation together on October 9. The weeks between mid-September and the start of radiation would be spent getting my house ready for my mom, helping her settle, organizing a schedule for all her appointments and medications, and anticipating my MRI coming up on October 19. But if I did not start figuring out more ways to take care of myself other than hydrating, I may not even make it to the MRI. My next step was to get much smarter about my eating habits.

NOURISH

Once you get drinking enough water to become a habit (and you will) then you can move onto another easy step like healthy snacking. Let's be realistic here – if you are living the hospital life, you are likely not going to be banking on three square meals a day. Do not do what I did in the beginning and allow yourself to starve all day, therefore increasing your craving-driven likelihood to stop by a fast-food restaurant on your way home and stuff yourself with highly saturated fatty crap. Treat your hospital life as a day job and pack yourself some health-conscious snacks or a lunch.

I will allow myself bragging rights here and say that I am a fantastic vegetable eater and always have been. I can thank my mom's complete three-time cover to cover readings of *Fit for Life* when I was four years old for the success of a childhood where I was taught the value of healthy food and eating from the earth. Admittedly though, in my most tumultuous days, when the world was spinning under my feet and I had no clue which way was forward, I became guilty of getting caught in the hurricane that was rushing out the door unprepared for the day and living on cheese-crusted croissants. However, as I mentioned above with the water, the right foods will raise your frequency too, so start eating higher.

Where to start? Aim for colourful – not colourful wrappers, but colourful foods. If you are going to snack, at least make it nutrient-rich and not just calorie-rich. Preparing fresh vegetables by cutting them up and throwing them into small containers when I could find a quiet moment at home helped me. If you are cooking dinner, cut extra veggies then and get them into baggies or containers so that they are ready to grab and toss into your bag in the mornings.

Make protein your best friend. Look for a good quality protein powder. I love plant-based powders. A simple protein drink is a great way to hydrate and feed your body at the same time. Maybe it will end up replacing one of your mid-day coffees. Look for a few healthy protein bar options and even keep a few stashed in your car to avoid the fast-food stop on the way home. Protein helps keep your body satiated longer and therefore helps decrease cravings for sugary sweets. Get acquainted.

Look for things like hummus, which can accompany your fresh veggies to ensure you are getting a good load of protein each day.

Let's face it – the ride is an emotional rollercoaster on its best days. There will be days where you will end up eating your feelings but if you have set yourself up for an otherwise healthy day, or week, then you can enjoy those feeling-eating-binges as a treat and not beat yourself up for them. If you are making the stop for the greasy burger and fries, then skip the soda, sip the water, and save some money.

SLEEP AND REST

I will not pretend that I think you are getting enough sleep. I know I did not and rarely still do. Unless you are my mother, she was a magical creature who would be asleep as her head hit the pillow and then not move a muscle from the position that she had started in all night long. I know this to be especially true from the months that she lived with me, and I had developed a nightly routine of having to walk right up close to her as she slept to ensure she was even still breathing.

Some nights the mental and physical toll of not sleeping would stress me out so much that I would not sleep. You can spiral into ironic cycles where you are so worried about not getting enough sleep that the worry turns into anxiety, and you cannot calm yourself down enough to sleep. You already have enough things and worries keeping you up at night so do not make sleep one of them.

As a little girl, I remember having those terrible nights where it would take me what felt like hours to fall asleep. I know we have all experienced this and still do as adults. I would stare at the ceiling, forever wondering if it was possible to not sleep at all for an entire night. Of course, I always fell asleep eventually, but my mom would comfort me by telling me to focus on rest instead of actual sleep. She would patiently remind me that resting my body and being still was just as important as falling asleep and so not to worry or stress, but to focus on closing my eyes, taking deep breaths, and thinking good thoughts.

You are likely not going to be having beautiful, serene, eight-hour slumbers even though we both know that is the dream and that is what we believe our body truly needs. If it is not happening, shift your focus to giving your body the quiet, beneficial rest it requires and stop stressing out so much about REM cycles because that is serving nobody – ever.

My mom taught me this other incredibly valuable trick as a girl to help me fall asleep, and while we have a million tricks like counting sheep or focusing on breath, this one serves double duty. She would have me name three things that I was grateful for in my day. The key here is to not just think about them, but to bask in them. Focus on them. Relive them. Feel them in your bones and in your heart. Was it a hug from your parent? A look they gave you where you saw their soul? Was it an uncle bringing you another round of fresh hot coffee? Were you proud that you packed yourself some decent snacks Perhaps relieved that a stranger dropped off a meal? You heard good news on the radio? Your mom swallowed her oral chemo pills, and you didn't find them dissolving in the bottom of her juice cup? Feel it all. Breathe it in. Count at least three things in your day and one of two things will happen: either you will fall asleep, or you will keep going down the happy gratitude rabbit hole and raise your frequency and restfulness in the process. Win-win.

By September 18, my mom was able to go home. With my stepfather being a struggling alcoholic and the fact that he had planned to continue working full time, Kenny and I had made the easy decision to open our home up to my mom. Due to my parents' heightened risk of seizures, neither one of them was supposed to be left alone and both had lost their licenses. They would require daily transportation to the hospital and full-time care as they recovered from brain surgeries and took on daily doses of radiation. I would put my landscaping business into the hands of my capable staff, shelf my Beautycounter consultant business temporarily, and lower my commitments for the mom coaching podcast I was well into recording season two of with my good friend Theresa.

I would stop it all and take care of my parents the best way that I could with whatever time I may have left. My mom would stay with me Monday to Friday and then go home to spend weekends with her husband.

On September 18th, my dad also had his first appointment at the General Hospital across town for a consultation with the radiation oncologist. Dr. Nair was also spearheading a

clinical trial in which both parents had volunteered to partic-
ipate. After the appointment, my dad and Jackie bounced
back over to the Civic to visit me, Rich, my mom, and Marc
again. To our surprise, Dr. Nair had followed them. He had
also bounced from one hospital to another, going from an
appointment with my dad to then come and meet my mom,
his newest glioblastoma patient. They would start radiation
together, on the same day, with the same doctor in the same
trial. I would now spend their journey comparing one
against the other as trial subjects.

I stepped out into the hall to greet my dad and Jackie
before they came into the room and was caught by surprise
by the swelling in my dad's face. Above his right temple, a
wobbly bubble of fluid had built up. It jiggled slightly when
touched and instantly reminded me of the waterbed my
parents shared when we were young. Jackie seemed
concerned by it and decided to walk my dad down the hall to
the nurse practitioner's office. Paul, the nurse practitioner,
took one look and suggested that they head straight down to
the emergency neuro clinic on the second floor to be
assessed. This did not look promising. My stomach dropped
again while they excused themselves to go be seen by a
neurologist, leaving me frightened again for his health and
having to collect my nerves enough to turn and head back
into my mom's room where Dr. Nair waited for me with a
manilla file labelled, 'Matthews, Christine.'

We each leaned around the perimeter of her bed, allowing
the metal bed rails to support our weight as Dr. Nair
confirmed that both of my mom's tumors were glioblastoma.
This was it. We would officially have one year with both.
Maybe.

We packed up my mom, her belongings, and what was left
of our hearts, shortly after Dr. Nair left the room and helped
her into a wheelchair to take her to her car. I had let my

seven-year-old daughter, Ryann, tag along with me that day. Since her birthday, three-quarters of a month prior, things had been a whirlwind and she was missing her grandparents badly. She had asked if she could push Granny in the wheelchair and out to the car and I had let her, with some guidance and redirecting. I marveled at her physical strength in pushing and steering this bulky device when she was not even tall enough to see over my mom's freshly scarred head and tattered, blood-crusted hair. And I realized another key component I would require in taking care of two grown dependents: a body that could handle it.

MOVE YOUR BODY

This goes without saying, but caregiving can get physical. If you were terminally ill and lying in a bed, would you choose the unhealthy-looking, sleep-deprived, unstable nurse to aid in lifting you from your bed to your wheelchair or would you choose the smiling, energetic, well-rested, vibrant, and strong-looking nurse? Do not be that first option for them. Be the one they would choose.

This does not mean that anyone needs to drop pounds or start lifting heavy or join a gym, but simply that you need to keep your body moving, agile, and capable. Hydrating and feeding yourself is certainly the best way to start but now that you are loving your body that way, get moving.

Time may not be on your side if you are trying to haul a household out the door each morning and barely remembering to grab your water bottle and snacks on your way so gym or basement workouts may not seem like a viable option for you, and that is okay. But do what you can do. Start each morning, after your ten deep breaths, with a few stretches before you get moving. Throw in three sets of ten body squats while you brush your teeth (I have pulled this one out on many occasions). While you are feeding them lunch, stand instead of sitting and do a few calve raises. Sitting at a red light on your way to the hospital, straighten up your posture and pull your belly button into your lower back, hold it for a count of two, slowly release, and repeat until the light turns green.

Your body is going to be called on for a lot of physical things as a caregiver so take care of it. No matter what physical size or shape you are in, love your body enough to keep it moving and your blood flowing from that great big heart of yours so that you are the person your parents choose and trust to keep them safe.

DRESS THE PART

You do not need to buy a new wardrobe. In fact, don't. Unless that is your coping mechanism then do what you need to do and that is a completely different book. But do dress sensibly. Scrubs exist for a reason. A caregiver needs to be able to move freely and comfortably. Wear shoes that will support you being on your feet for most of the day on hard and unforgiving concrete floors. It only took me two fourteen-hour hospital days in cute flip-flops to realize what a bad idea that was. Be comfy and confident.

You are not going to get paid for this new role but treat it as if you will. Show up for the part and for your parent in a way that shows them you are there for them and that their care means the world to you. First and foremost, as a parent myself, I know that my dream for my babies is that they learn to take care of themselves. I have spent my parenting life thus far role modelling that for them. Imagine the gift it is to your parent to see you taking care of yourself so that you can take care of them.

That is love coming full circle.

6

GET ORGANIZED

The day my dad came home from this first surgery was September 4. While I scurried around his hospital room that morning, packing up all his belongings, Jackie was chatting with his nurse practitioner, Paul. The two of them huddled over the window ledge. Jackie frantically tried to follow his directions on medication and timing and dosages. She was scribbling notes all over the printed forms he was combing through with her to try to collect her thoughts and herself into a means of language that she would understand – short-hand margin scribbles.

There were somewhere around fourteen new medications for him to take. That was his parting gift. Not only that, but none of those meds would be leaving the hospital that day with them. Jackie would now be responsible to get her wobbly freshly healing husband home and then was on her own to get to the pharmacy in good time to fill all those prescriptions and have them back home in time for him to take them as per the scheduled time. But wait. Wasn't he not supposed to be left alone? Was she supposed to drag him all over the pharmacy with her?

Paul handed her another list – this one with doctor appointments, blood workups, consultations, preliminary work for radiation, preliminary work for the clinical trial he had been approved for, follow-up appointment with the neurosurgeon, and all spanning over three different hospitals. Jackie looked lost. I could feel the overwhelm oozing out of her from across the room as I carefully packed his laptop into his computer bag. *How the heck was she expected to take care of all of this?*

Then my phone lit up. I reached across to my dad's bedside table to get it and saw that it was a text from my mom asking if we knew yet what time my dad was going to be discharged. She was checking in and feeling heartbroken that the once love of her life had had to endure all of this – the pain, the fear, the prognosis. She wished more than anything that she could be at the hospital each day to hug me and Richard, hug Jackie and my dad, ensure us all that we would all be okay. On that day, my mom was still at work, unknowingly sporting two deadly tumors in her head.

I told her that we were packing up his stuff, made note of the insane list of medications and appointments that Jackie had just been slapped with, and responded with a "Looks like I'm making a stop at Indigo to get Jackie a calendar on my way to dad's." She was going to need it. And that is exactly what I did.

When we got my dad inside their house, I patiently settled him onto the couch, propping him with more pillows than were necessary and tucking him with blankets. He looked like a baby. I thought about the irony of how this was the other way around for the first thirty-six years. Now we would reverse roles.

Jackie right away got her new calendar open and started slotting in his appointments. They spanned weeks and had no rhyme or reason, or even shared locations.

The very first appointment listed was to meet the oncologist, Dr. Nicholas.

Oh God, I thought, *that's the one where he will finally know the prognosis.* My stomach did a back flip. I could not bear the thought of what that was going to feel like. However, I reminded myself that on that day I would also be meeting my mom for a birthday lunch and a little shopping. There was something good that would still come out of that day. No matter how hard that appointment was going to be, my mom would be there afterward to remind me that I still had her. She would hug me tightly and melt away some of the pain.

Jackie continued to write the appointments in, filling the calendar all the way up until the end of December. She then ducked out with her grocery list of prescriptions and headed to the pharmacy while I put on a movie and cuddled up beside my dad, trying hard not to stare at the forty-two metal staples snaking along in his head. I asked him how he was feeling every thirty-nine seconds or so. He probably wanted me to go home.

Jackie returned with a bag of bottles and a second bag of clear plastic pill organizers. This woman was on it. It seemed that her calendar and organized pill containers had allowed her a much better sense of control. I felt immediately grateful for her former experience in the medical world. Her years of nursing school and caregiver training were now coming in handy and her ability to organize and cut the required pills with such precision mesmerized me. *What would any regular untrained person do?* I wondered. *What would I do?*

Three days later was my thirty-seventh birthday. When my dad and Jackie arrived, Jackie had her schedule and his pill boxes in tow. She was in control, but looked run-down, exhausted, depleted, scared. All I could do was hug her and feel the comfort in knowing that she somewhat knew what the hell she was doing. But even she, trained and capable and familiar with Latin medicinal terms, was spent. Who in the heck was going to take care of her if it took everything in her to take care of my dad?

While we ate our ice-cream cake and I watched Jackie nervously encourage my dad for twelve straight minutes to take his metformin pill (the steroids were throwing him into full-blown diabetes), my mom was across the city in her own home having a seizure.

On the afternoon of September 18, I found myself hunched over my place at the window ledge while the same nurse practitioner, Paul, went over the same list of medications and a fresh new appointment schedule tailored just for my mom but containing all the same doctor's names as my dad's. I thought of Jackie and knew that Marc and I would also need to get organized quick. I had double the number of appointments to keep track of. My mom was being discharged in a few hours and in two days would be coming to spend the weeks with me.

I was no longer just an accompaniment or support to Jackie and my dad at his appointments. I would now become the chauffeur, the personal support worker, the pill cutter, the drug pusher, the personal assistant for my mom. I needed my own damn calendar from Indigo.

As life of a caregiver to my mom and backup support for my dad intensified, life at home with three school-age kids did not slow down either. Some days I forgot about picking up my kids from school because went into the hospital for an appointment at noon and got stuck needing to do extra blood work or paperwork or a doctor ran late putting us two hours behind schedule

Social media post from October 9, 2019:

"The hospital is like quicksand. It sucks you in and keeps you there for as long as it can. Just when you think your appointment is over and all went smoothly and you head for the sunlight beaming in through the front doors, singing your name, something was missed, some nurse needs to see you, some bloodwork was forgotten and back down you go, deeper and deeper until the hope of reaching the sunlight and the crisp fall air can no longer be seen. It is always something. There are so many hands in the pot in a situation like this (times two) that something always comes up. On the days where you say, *"Maybe we will get to just walk in, get treated and leave*, the hospital hears you, laughs and manifests some reason to turn your quick visit into a minimum or three hours because that is apparently hospital standard."

It was hard not to be consumed by the number of appointments and extras. I was packing the water and the snap peas and the hummus but forgetting to pick up my kids. I was missing my appointments left, right, and center, and one day even forgot to take my daughter to a friend's birthday party that we had RSVP'd yes to weeks earlier.

I was trying to simultaneously oversee my landscaping company in some slight way, run my Beautycounter business, make it onto weekly training calls on Zoom, juggle my appointments as well as doctor and dentist appointments for the three kids and everyone's extracurriculars, including my own. (In our family those are almost all sports.) I was trying to keep so many balls in the air and dropping all of them.

On top of all of that, I was lost with how to productively prioritize even the smaller things in life like watering plants, doing laundry, responding to emails, or laughing with my kids, which no longer seemed to be just happening without it being planned. The caregiving life will completely consume you if you let it. Here are my go-to organization strategies that keep the storm brewing in your head to a dull roar.

BRAIN DUMP

Ironic choice of wording, isn't it? A brain dump has become one of my favourite times of the week. Once a week gift yourself the time for a brain dump. You will not regret it. I choose Sundays so that I am best set up to live my week with more intention. I make a fresh coffee, find somewhere quiet in my house, sit with a blank paper and a pen, and dump all thoughts out of my brain and onto paper. If you are type-A, this might look something like a neatly spaced, bullet-point list. If you are type-B (me), this may look like a colourful and messy brainstorm activity that you used to do back in elementary school. I break out different coloured pens and even draw a fluffy cloud around the words "Brain Dump" in the middle of my blank paper. Then, get to it, writing down everything you have on your to-do list, right down to painting the house siding or washing your face. Set a timer and allow yourself fifteen minutes for this exercise. Put it all on there, kids' sports, house stuff, social engagements, Netflix series you think you need to catch up on, phone calls you need to make, rooms that need to be vacuumed. Get it all out.

Then set another timer for fifteen minutes, sip your coffee or tea while it's still hot and delicious, and organize your list into three different columns.

- Urgent
- Delegate
- Later

Split this up into what needs to happen this week and what can realistically wait. Got your urgent list ready? Plunk it into small to-dos on your calendar. This will help you get that overwhelming and ever-growing swirling list of 'things' out of your head onto paper where they can be more prioritized and leave you space up top for more focus, gratitude, and love.

DELEGATE

You have dumped what was in your brain and categorized it; now it is time to give some of it away and put it into capable hands. What can you task out? On top of being an ass-kicking, kale-loving, hydrated guru of a caregiver in great sensible runners and with stronger legs than ever, you are now a project manager and the project is your life No project manager takes on all the tasks by themselves. They delegate. They find strengths in other people, and they lovingly dump all the things they suck at onto someone who is better equipped and reliable. Believe it or not, my eight-year-old daughter makes a pot of coffee for me every morning. One thing less for me to worry about.

I tried to do it all alone for way too long. I tried to be at the school for pickup every single day without fail while my recently radiated mom would sit in the car in the parking lot alone and wait for me to collect my brood. What she needed was to be back at my house resting. Even though she never complained about anything ever, the guilt was killing me. What I eventually decided to do was ask a few friends to pick my kids up at the end of the day a few days a week. The kids did not always love being picked up by other people. But it meant I could get my mom home for the rest she needed after radiation. I would be much less frazzled than I had been trying to drive from the hospital to school to home where I would unload three starving, whining kids with backpacks and a tired, confused, weak mom all at the same time.

I gave full scheduling of my landscaping business to my staff and let them sort it out completely on their own (and with raises). Taking that one bit of stress off my plate and knowing that my clients were in the most competent hands was such a weight off my shoulders.

I gave myself grace and permission to miss one of my hockey games if it was a day where I was just too rundown emotionally to get up off the floor. I had to learn how to cancel without guilting myself for being a terrible teammate. Not one person on my team, the girls that truly knew me, were ever anything but understanding. I gave myself that same grace and permission to let the kids miss one of their games or practices if they were not feeling it that day either.

Cancel when you just cannot do it and know that this is not the regular you, this is the survival mode caregiving you. Your goal cannot be to not let everyone else down. Your goal must be to never let yourself down. I promise you that by not letting yourself down, by coming from a place of genuinely putting your mental health first, you in turn will not let your parent down either.

MAKE A TOP FIVE

I live by lists. But life had tugged the rug out from under me so fast that I no longer felt I had the time to write "make a list" anywhere so that I could even remember to do it. My mind was unravelling fast, and I felt like I was disappointing everyone, especially myself. Small things that had not come up in my brain dump seemed to be popping up here and there.

I decided to take four minutes every night at bedtime to write a top four list on a Post-it pad before going to sleep/lying awake for hours practicing turning my worry into gratitude. I would write what I thought in that moment would be my five priorities from the "Urgent" column of my brain dump list for the next day, outside of scheduled appointments. Sometimes it was as little as, "Text Kristy." Other times they were bigger reminders like, "Pay the lawn company." Many times, it included questions to ask my parents' doctors, or worse, questions to ask my children's teachers as they were starting to fall behind. Often it was as simple as, "Take twenty minutes and play with the kids," "Kick a soccer ball with Ryann," "Read a book to Wesley."

Five is manageable. Five allows us to feel not only in control, but also productive. If you are a phone person, write your list in your notes app before bed. If you are a paper and pen generation like me, refusing to trust technology enough to move forward into this century, write it down. Leave a notepad beside your bed like it's 1995 and do this every night. Try your best to keep it to five, no more. Remember that if it did not make it onto the list, it did not need to be there.

You have enough to remember already with the water and the protein and the decent shoes and the hair ties and then you have the bonus, if you are still living hospital life every day, that just about anything can change at any given moment and throw you for a loop so be gentle with yourself and keep your expectations low. Your goal right now is survival and love. You cannot give, nor can you receive love if you are tapped out.

Shortly after my mom's diagnosis, Marc contacted their lawyer about getting their wills started. The hope and dream, I think, was that once my mom got home from the hospital, they would go out to see their lawyer together and get the will finalized. Between the fact that my mom was only home on weekends and the unfortunate nature of Marc's alcoholism, they never made it to the lawyers. This left Marc trying to juggle the will all on his own but with the mental space he was in he was able to cope with truly little other than working, crying, and drinking. Each time I asked Marc about it he would slough off the same, "Yeah, I'm just waiting for the lawyer to draft something up." To this day I am truly unsure whether he was feeding me a line to buy time or has honest to goodness the slowest lawyer known to mankind but regardless, I never felt I had a straight answer.

My mom's condition was quickly worsening. Both her cognitive and physical abilities were on a fast downward slide. One week into November my mom had already resorted to just sleeping on our couch. After several near falls down the stairs even she had come to realize that toppling backwards on top of me was not going to be good for anyone involved. Besides, she had become lazier and lazier in brain cancer life and no longer had the energy to put into standing, let alone stair climbing. She had been sleeping on the couch for three straight nights and had barely left that same spot for as many days, asides from daily radiation outings.

As her radiation went on, she declined faster and faster. On November 14, I woke her up from the couch, gave her a quick, keto-worthy breakfast, and left to get the kids to school. When I returned home, she was slumped completely over on her side and fast asleep, her empty breakfast plate balancing on her lap and threateningly close to crashing to the floor.

For a week she had needed me to follow her into the bathroom and help her take down and pull up her pants when she was finished. By the end of that week, I was physically lifting her off the toilet as well. And on this particular morning, after giving her breakfast on the couch, I let her lie back down for some more rest while I quickly whisked the kids off to school. When I got back home fifteen minutes later, she was asleep, so I left her that way while I quietly snuck upstairs, showered, and got ready for our radiation appointment later that morning. I then tried waking her again only to find she had fallen asleep with a mouthful of her breakfast. When I woke her, she did not seem to have a clue that her mouth had anything in it. She also could not hold her body upright on the couch and with every attempt I made to safely sit her up, she would slump back over onto her side. After an hour of trying everything that I could to help her, I excused myself upstairs, succumbed to the threat of tears and made the difficult decision to call 911 with a head full of fear and a heart full of sorrow. *Was this going to be it?*

She was bounced from hospital to hospital for ten days and diagnosed with hydrocephalus, a build-up of fluid on the brain. We were told she would need a shunt and that surgery would be imminent. Of course, surgery was not imminent, and the story changed every day from doctor to doctor. She had three radiation appointments left and one doctor thought it would be best for her to head back to the Cancer Center as an inpatient and complete her last three rounds of radiation.

Less than two weeks later, I had scheduled a meeting with her new radiation oncologist, the social worker, and my mom's husband. It was decided by doctors over the two weeks since I called the ambulance, that this was going to be as good as it would get. It was time to make the decision on where she should be placed next. *Where she would go to die*, was exactly how it translated to me. My stomach turned at the thought. A meeting was required to make some gut-wrenching and hard decisions, decisions I thought I still had a year to avoid. Our meeting was on a Monday at 10:00 a.m. I had not slept the night before. I had likely not even slept the night before that one. Or the eighty-eight nights before that. It was all happening so fast. There was supposed to be so much more to this. The realization that the quintessential "If you only had one year to live" question and the idealistic ways we would spend that

– travelling, partying, reveling – was not going to happen
for us.

It was shortly after 6:00 a.m. when my phone flashed its
blue light, waking me up. It was a text from my stepdad
confirming the time of the meeting. "It's at 10:00." I was
relieved that neither of us would have to face this alone. I
was relieved that he had stopped drinking again because I
needed so desperately to rely on him.

I dropped the kids off at school that morning, got a coffee
for the road, (water bottles and snacks already packed, of
course) and headed straight to my mom. I had arrived early
and had a few minutes to chat with her before the meeting.
She asked why we would be meeting with the doctors when
she was going to be going home that weekend. My heart
sank. These questions and comments from her had become
pretty regular about going back home due to her confusion
about her physical state. She could not understand that her
brain had stopped telling her legs how to work. She would
likely never walk again.

The appointment time came. My stepdad did not.
Another five minutes slowly rolled by. My stepdad did not.
My stomach dropped. He was not coming. I knew in my
heart that he had started drinking again. The sober version
of my stepdad would have positively been here. He would
not have let me do this alone. I was filling with devastation
and rage.

I sat through that meeting alone, making decisions about
whether she wanted to be resuscitated if her heart stopped, if
she would want to be cremated, and other impossible decisions that I knew my catholic mother would have had defi-
nite faith-based opinions on but was too far gone for me to
ask. I did it alone, wishing more than anything that one
single soul would have been in that room with me to validate
my choices.

When he finally made it to the hospital later that afternoon, he broke down in sobs in the hallway outside of my mom's room. He admitted to me that he had drunk so much the night before that he had woken up at 6:00 a.m. still intoxicated, texted me, and went back to sleep. When he woke again later in the morning, he was in no condition to drive. By the sight of him and the conversation we were having in the hallway he was still in no way to have driven, and the rage roared again as I pictured all the ways he could have screwed up more lives than just ours with his drinking and driving. I wished I had known he would get in a car still in an intoxicated state and drive the forty minutes to the hospital. I wish I had known and called the police.

He broke down about having screwed up. He broke down about how he could not go on without her. He broke down about how he had come close to ending it all the night before. The grief for him, life without the person that gave him reason to get out of bed every morning, had become more than he could bear. The need to self-soothe had become stronger than his will to carry on. This happens with addiction. It does not allow the individual to find, use or strengthen the tools needed to cope. Therefore, I knew again, that I could only rely on myself.

The will had not been finalized and we were running out of time. Without a will, I was left to take my best guess and chose things for my mom's end-of-life care with the most empathy and compassion for her I could muster. I left the hospital that afternoon and phoned her lawyer myself, explaining that I was advocating for my mom. He came out to the hospital the next day, will in hand, no questions asked.

WILLS

I know. We all think it is gross. Many of us squirm at the thought of planning our death or life on this planet without us in it. It. Is. Weird. But it is wildly important and wildly comforting. Let's just have the conversation, okay?

When my dad was diagnosed, he and Jackie had no will. With him being a number-crunching, budget-loving, money guy, I was shocked. When my mom was diagnosed right after, she and Marc had no will either. My parents had a will when they were together but had not created new ones with their new spouses whom they had each been with for more than seventeen years. There was no excuse for this.

Whether you are reading this book as the patient or as the caregiver or as the person who heard about my compelling story and had to read it for yourself, go get your will done if you do not already have one. Losing a parent is hard enough. Losing a parent and having to guess about what they wanted done with their remains, assets, estates, and stuff is a whole new level of hard.

A basic will through a lawyer can take several weeks and be costly, especially if you have many assets or dependents to work into the mix. But it is an investment that will save those same children (or any loved one) a world of heartache at a time when the heartache is already so heavy.

You can purchase will kits online for less. Or at the least, write your wishes down on paper, sign it, save it somewhere special, and tell someone where it is. Even that will hold up in a court of law. But outside of law and money, as a child of a parent who died intestate (without a will), I cannot express how difficult it has been making decisions for my mother about DNRs, cremation, even location of burial, on a guess and a prayer. I cannot go backwards but the second-guessing will always exist. I will always wonder if I made the right decisions for her.

Back to the law side of things, dying intestate will put your money where you may not have wanted your money to go. If you are going to or have worked hard your whole life to be able to have something to pass down to your children or to donate to your favourite charity, you want the security of knowing that those wishes will happen for you, so get them on paper, properly. Do not let the burden of that guessing game fall upon someone else's shoulders the way it fell upon mine.

If your parent does not have an up-to-date will, help them to get that done. Yes, this is a lot of work for you. Call in backup if needed. Look into a death doula. Death doulas are becoming an increasingly popular way to go as they are trained to hold your hand all the way through the dying process, from helping you find counselling, to telling family and making medical decisions, wills, and funeral arrangements. Delegate out phone calls to siblings if they are responsible enough. Lawyers will come right to the hospital to get things signed on-site if need be, so there is no excuse.

While my dad and Jackie went right away the week after he was home from his first hospital visit and got their wills done, my mom did not as I have just shared. I called her lawyer to come and have the will signed one day in the hospital. He drove an hour into the city just to deem her "not of sound mind" and she was not able to sign the will. Nothing in her case has been easy.

There is a time and money commitment here but love yourself and your parent enough to make sure theirs is done and then do yours.

The schedule and demands of hospital life are going to be ever-changing. Taking a large portion of worry off your plate with wills is monumental. Using the brain dump activity, schedule yourself a small chunk of time (thirty minutes should do it) and sit quietly, even if beside their hospital bed, where you can have some space to listen to what is in your head and get it on paper. Then, getting comfortable with delegating some of those tasks out will ease your mind and take the extra burden off you. With what is left, give yourself the ritual of taking five minutes every night to choose five of the things on your list that you think you can realistically manage the next day. (Hint: no one needs to be married to this. The list can change throughout the day as your day changes.)

Lastly, cross things off. Something happens on an energetic level when you can physically cross off the things you have accomplished, even if it was "brush teeth." In a world where you stare at drab creamy hospital walls with the humming and beeping soundtrack of monitors and possible moans from down the hall in the background, you need to build off the energy of every accomplishment you possibly can, big or small. Go, you. Cross it off, feel the energetic shift. And maybe make one of those four things celebrating yourself in all your accomplished and caregiving awesomeness. Love is in the details.

7

CREATE YOUR ENVIRONMENT

For every day that I forgot a school pick-up – as we went over in the last chapter, not my finest moment – someone was there. I have the incredible blessing of belonging to a circle of mom friends from my children's school and together we can pick each other up when one of us is down. This is something that every human being needs, but especially mothers. It takes a village, as they say, and they are not wrong. Part of this process for you is going to be learning who your village is and even more importantly, who your village is not.

On any given day, if I did not show up at the school, one of them just took my children back to their house until I can get there. And in the case of my parents' diagnoses, it was a no-questions-asked situation. They were not interested in details or excuses; they simply understood that I was up to my eyeballs in pill chopping and steric strips and that my kids needed to get home safe. Now do not get me wrong, until our world was tipped off its axis with these brain cancers, I picked up my children every day after school without fail. The tumultuous uncertainties of hospital life, however, threw me off my schedule. Simply put I just could not do it alone.

ACCEPT HELP

One day my daughter's teacher, who also happened to be a friend and neighbour, dropped the kids off for me after school. When she came to the door she said, "Laura, I want you to go upstairs and bring me all of your laundry. I am going to do your laundry and I am not leaving here without it." I did not argue. I went upstairs, got the heaping basket from our walk-in closet, sifted through and removed all the underwear and other embarrassing items and brought her a basket consisting of mainly towels and socks. She looked at me and said, "Laura, you have six people living in this house right now. I know for a fact that this is not all your laundry. I am going to put this in my car and when I come back to your door, I want to see at least two more baskets."

It was humbling and a hard way to learn to accept help on a level that I had not before. Having my friends pick up my kids from school, accepting revolving drop-offs of hot meals, coming home to cards stuffed in my mailbox and gift bags hanging off the front door – those were one thing, but allowing someone else to wash my dirty undies, that was a whole other. I stuffed the underwear back into the next basket, ran through each kid's room collecting their soiled hampers, and brought them all down to Krista. She never so much as flinched. She just smiled, thanked me, and turned to take them to her car.

Thanked me.

How the hell was she thanking me for a basket full of thongs and dirty kid socks? Because she finally found a way to help. People *want* desperately to help you. The problem is that typically they have no clue how. How many times do you hear people say, "I don't know how I can help you," "What do you need?" "Let me know if there is anything I can do?"

People feel weird around death and terminal illness and if they have not experienced it to the level of caregiving that you are providing, then they just do not know how to offer their support and so they shy away. When Krista had a light-bulb moment realizing that she could wash some clothes, she felt good. As humbling as it was for me, it was equally as heart filling to watch her light up at the idea of helping someone else. I just needed to remind myself that she wore underwear too. As human beings, our job is to help those in need but so often, we are beating our heads against the wall trying to figure out what that looks like. If they do figure something out, then our job, as the sufferer, is to let them.

After my mom's diagnosis, a few of my friends set up a meal train. They had requested that the meals provide enough food for not only my family of five, but also to cover my parents, stepparents, and brother. Every day Kenny or I would come home to a cooler outside our front door packed with that night's dinner and often an extra treat or some extra baking for the kids for the week. Then Kenny or I would get to plating and heating it up and portioning the rest into containers that I could bring to the rest of my family the next day.

This meal train was made up of 50 percent strangers. People I had never met before, cooking homemade and delicious meals for my family. Using their time, resources, money, and skills to make a moment in our lives easier. Often, I would even come home to find gift cards left by strangers, or anonymously, waiting for me by my front door.

The week before the kids started school, only days after my dad had been diagnosed, I had put a post on social media about school supplies. I did not have the capacity in the heat of the diagnosis and living at the hospital awaiting, during, and recovering from surgery to scroll through my emails to find the one with the kids' school lists and then go shop for the supplies and get the kids organized. The guilt was setting in hard. My post had asked for someone to send me a short supply list.

Shortly after my post went up, my cousin's wife, Paula, texted me to tell me that she was heading out to do the shopping for me and would use the school board provided lists. Of course, I tried to fight her on this and of course, she would hear none of it. She showed up later that evening armed with three large shopping bags. One for each kid and each containing one of every single item on the supplies list. The kids were elated. I asked her how much and got my phone to electronically transfer her the money and she informed me that her mother, who lived all the way on the other side of Canada had paid for it all.

I looked at Paula, my jaw dropped to the floor, and I cried. I am not sure if I were more emotional over her and her mom's generosity or because of the relief that I would get to cross one more thing off my list and not have to worry about it. I relented that I could not let her mom pay for that even though I had appreciated the thought so much and that I would pay her back. Paula looked straight at me with both love and pleading and said, "Laura, there is literally an army of people out there that so desperately want to help. Put them to work."

Find your army. Open your heart up and let them in. Give them your grocery lists and your filthy laundry baskets and put them to work. They *want* to help. Love yourself enough to let them.

The thing about creating your army is that you must be willing to put the cry out for help. Here is a literal post I put up one evening when I felt like the walls of my home were closing in on me and I needed to get out, see people, feel the love and support that I knew my soul needed.

"This is an SOS. If anyone is free, I need to get out of the house, out of these walls, and be around familiar faces. Please come and save me from myself."

Certainly not my most shining moment but vulnerable enough to yield nearly thirty immediate direct messages and offers. Now, I went with the first offer I got which was a few of my hockey teammates willing not only to spend the evening with me but to come and pick me up and take me out of the house so that I did not have to worry about driving anywhere – a true break.

If you need help (and I am telling you that you do) then you must step up and say so. There is great strength in vulnerability. There is truly little strength in pretending you can do it on your and then crumbling. That will not do you or your parent any good. The beautiful gift in accepting help from others is that it gives you back the one single thing that you want more of with your loved one – time.

LOSE THE JOY SUCKERS

On the opposite end of accepting the help and creating your army of angels, you need to learn to eliminate what I like to refer to as "joy suckers." No matter what you do, no matter how pure and genuine you are being, haters gonna hate. It is gross and annoying. We wish that they just did not exist in our world, but they do and so let's feel heaps of sorry for them because they are obviously struggling in deeper ways than we can understand and let's just move on.

My mom had a friend (and I now question how genuinely I use that word for her) who loved my mom until it seemed my mom became physically unlovable. This friend, who I will call Sheila, loved her, doted over her, came to visit her in the hospital and coiffed her hair all nice until my mom's hair fell out. Weeks later, while my mom was living at my house, I posted a journal post on social media about the startling realization that my mom was starting to lose her beautiful, thick hair. I accompanied the post with a picture of the handful of hair front and center with her thinning head slightly blurred in the background.

"You know those moments in your life that you just know are going to etch themselves into your memory and stay there forever? And I'm not talking about sunsets on beaches or scaling the peaks of mountains. I am talking about the uniquely beautiful, the ugly, the raw and then real-life moments that you may or may not have seen coming. Tonight, I had one. It wasn't one I wanted. It walks a thin and high tightrope between ugly and beautiful, but it was definitely hard. I stood over my mom, applying Polysporin to her two incisions while she sat still on the bed checking a few emails on her phone. I parted her hair along each scar and ran my finger along the bumps and indents to leave a thin layer of ointment. It is less hard to do now, no staples, fewer scabs, a thinner line. But tonight, as I lifted and parted her hair, it became caught between my fingers and came out in handfuls.

I stood silently, hands tangled in hair, heat rising from my body, wondering if I should address it or pretend nothing happened and let her figure it out for herself tomorrow morning in the shower. I opted for honesty, no matter how uncomfortable. I decided that she needed to hear it from me in case she needed to cry, be angry, or laugh. But in the true nature of my mom, she just shrugged and said, "Oh well. It will grow back." She is stoic like that. She is my hero. And soon she will be my bald hero.

Sheila did not approve. The next morning, I received a private message questioning what my mom – a woman who took so much pride in her hair and appearance – would have thought about that, with a suggestion that I allow my mother to still have some dignity.

Days later, on another post that was too uncomfortable for Sheila to see because of *her* internal struggles, I got another private message from her about how I should at least have enough respect for my mother to put some lipstick on her first and comb her hair before posting pictures of her.

This list grew and grew. Every week or so I would get another message about how I was disrespecting my mom and stripping her of what dignity she had left. Sheila believed that hair and makeup made dignity and that dignity made the person. One week before Christmas, Sheila messaged me to tell me that she would no longer be able to visit my mom because it was too hard for her to see her like that but that she would continue to pray for her. I then started praying harder for Sheila.

Let's remember that we are not all cut from the same cloth. If you are reading this as someone who has stepped into the role of a caregiver for your parent, you are doing God's work. And, in a beautiful circle-of-life kind of way, this is exactly how your journey here started. They did God's work for you. They loved you wholeheartedly, clothed you, fed you, guided you, and accepted you. And now here you are, just seeing each other from reciprocal angles.

For people like Sheila, they have yet to accept that death is a part of living, and so they will continue to struggle to see images of it and will take that out on the people who are portraying it rather than coming to terms with it on their own. Remind yourself in these moments when others call into question your choices regarding your parents' care and how you handle it, that their issues with you have literally nothing to do with you.

The days had cooled toward the end of September. A new

lightness and crispness had settled into the air and the shorter amount of sunlight was drawing summer to a close. The clinical trial that both of my parents had heroically signed up for required a lot of blood work and paperwork and we were all back there together, on a Friday, getting the preliminary forms filled out. As we sat in the waiting room together, still unnerved by the trueness of that statement – together – Jackie's cell rang. Our adorable clinical trial manager, Alisar, was calling with the great news that my dad had been randomly placed into the test group. This trial was separating participants into two separate groups – a test group who would receive the new intravenous chemo-therapy drug, and those who would not. However, there was no placebo. You knew you were getting it, or you knew you were not getting it. There was no method to who would be placed into which group. We were told it was random selection.

We clapped and hugged at the news that my dad would be receiving the standard treatment as well as the new treat-ment. This was promising news. A little extra ray of hope. Then another horrific feeling settled around us all, weighing our elevated moods to the floor. What if my mom did not get placed in the same group? We all fell awkwardly silent and tried to carry on as if the phone call had never happened. I struggled with what to do with feelings so big and so polar-ized in having one parent hit what felt like the jackpot of brain cancer and the idea of the other potentially being robbed the opportunity by chance. We continued with our long waiting room stays and our bloodwork and our binders full of health forms until my parents were devoid of fluids and Jackie and I were devoid of emotion.

On Fridays, my aunt met me and my mom at the Cancer Center after radiation appointments and drove her back to her home on the western outskirts of town while I headed back to the east end to get the kids from school. My mom then spent two days at her home with Marc and then was dropped off again to me on Sundays at noon.

When my aunt Barb arrived, I had already pulled my car up to the front door to wait for her so that I could transfer my mom's suitcase and medicine bags easily to her. I helped my mom get safely into the car with her sister-in-law, told her that I loved her and kissed her cheek. Then I waved them off.

I got into my car and took a few minutes to settle myself before turning the key over in the ignition. The lights flicked to life on the dashboard – 3:10 p.m. I would barely make it to the school on time for pick up if I did not leave then. As my foot gently pushed the break and my hand reached for the gear shift, my phone sang its ringing song. It was Alisar. My stomach ended up again in my throat and I worried that if I answered right away it would block my voice and I would not be able to make any sound. I cleared my throat and answered.

After exchanging a few pleasantries, she cut to the chase, "I'm so sorry, Laura. I know that this is not the news that you want, and I wish this had happened differently, but your mom is in the control group. She will not receive the trial drug."

I would, without a shadow of a doubt and in every literal sense, spend the rest of their journeys unethically comparing one against the other and managing questions from others about who is faring better, due to science. We received many thoughts and opinions from people who were not them or their caregivers, people who were not facing brain cancer or a terminal diagnosis, about whether the trial was a good idea. My parents' thoughts on it, "Best-case scenario, it saves my life. Worst-case scenario, I help more people going forward."

I could not move. How would I tell her? I broke down crying. Then forgot to pick up my kids.

DO WHAT COMES NATURALLY AND IGNORE THE REST

When I was expecting my first daughter, Leightyn, I was given a card at my baby shower from my sister-in-law that simply read, in her handwriting, "Do what comes naturally and ignore the rest." Julie, a mom of two boys and one stepson, knew a thing or two about parenting by then. What she knew was that everybody was going to have an opinion about how you feed, sleep train, read to, love, swaddle, diaper, and talk to your baby. Her words made their way into my heart and head and always stayed with me. Those words gave me, a young mom-to-be about to embark on the terrifyingly subjective journey of motherhood, the innate superpower to block out everyone else's opinions of how I should raise my child, and just raise her.

I applied this to my parents when they got sick. This was not always the easiest thing to do. People's words, especially when they are continuous, are eventually going to get in. In those cases, simply sit with them quietly, feel them wholly, make a list of all the reasons why what they are saying may not make sense for you in your situation, and remind yourself of all the times you have trusted your intuition and it has worked out for you.

Your intuition is doing what comes naturally. It is not something that you have to think about. Remind yourself that you are an adult, you are here, you are breathing and have managed to keep yourself healthy enough to be still on this planet. You are likely wearing pants, and sensible shoes, after reading Chapter 4. You have fed yourself today (put this book down and do it now if you have not). Maybe you even showered. (Pat yourself on the back if you did this. I skipped this step on more days than I would like to admit). You even got yourself to the hospital, to your parent's house, wherever they may be. No one dragged you there kicking and screaming. You did this all on intuition and it led you this far. Keep listening to it. Stop listening to Sheila.

Another place where you are going to be inundated with incoming unsolicited advice is around the disease itself. If you have not been pummeled by the battering ram of well-intended friends and family sending you articles to check out on how eating pig's testicles can cure this type of disease but only when you pair it with a dandelion root salad and top it with mayonnaise, then strap on a helmet and brace yourself. You will get every article, clinical trial, new research publication, GoFundMes on other people dealing with similar illnesses (or not similar at all) coming to an inbox near you. These are not bad things. These are all great things. But these are just way too many things.

If you are anything like me (an over-committed people pleaser), I am assuming that you do not have boatloads of extra time to read in between treatment appointments, meal prepping, possible parent diaper changes, and checking the bottom of their drink cup to see if any of their pills even went in their mouths. And did you cross the eleven-city-block spread of the hospital and walk the plank and down to the bowels of the basement and around the backup generator to find the tiny parking office to get your new parking pass for the month yet? Or are you still paying $20 like a sucker because it barely seems worth the trek when the hospital has already sucked you in, turning your mom's twenty-minute radiation appointment into a full-fledged blood-sucking, sodium-level testing, four-hour type of day? And now you are late to pick up her latest chemo prescription from the pharmacy and fear she may die on your watch. But did you read that article I sent?

I want to be quite clear that I am not demoralizing anyone sending articles. I have been an article-sender too. But I am willing to guess that when you do find yourself basking in the luxury of a spare twenty minutes or so, you are probably reading a book you enjoy or researching something related to the disease on your own. I am saying this to relieve you of the pressure you may feel to keep up with these opinions that are coming at you and to remind you that you will not disappoint anyone by simply not reading them all. Thank the sender, let them know how much you love them for loving you, and get on with your brain dump exercise.

When a terminal diagnosis is given, there is a sad but fairy-tale ideology that we may have one year left with them but dammit if we are going to let it pass by. We are going to do it up big. Book the cruise. Plan the party. Reserve all the fancy restaurants. Call the sky diving place. Make. This. Count.

The sad reality around a diagnosis of glioblastoma is that six months of that last year are going to be spent doing treatments if you are lucky. The most successful glioblastoma patient stories get years and years after that. But there aren't many such stories. In the case of my mom, as you know, two months after her diagnosis she landed back in the hospital again and never came out.

Sheila visited her at the Civic Hospital the day before she was transferred back to the Cancer Center. When I told Sheila about the doctor's latest plan to have my mom finish her last three radiation treatments, she was outraged and told me not to let them continue this and to just let her die in peace. But Sheila was one person, an outsider, who had only shown up with opinions but was not the one in the ring with my mom. As controversial as it may be, I made the decision to trust the doctors.

Sheila chose not to see my mom again after that, as I mentioned earlier in this chapter. The reality of my mom's decline was too hard for her. When people say that, I wonder if they think that I am over here having a picnic. My mom was transferred back to the Cancer Center the following morning and continued the treatments that week. And you know the rest; the treatments made no difference, and we were informed by a new doctor that this was going to be as good as it would get for her. She would now need to be moved to a continuing care hospital where she could receive around-the-clock care and chemotherapy would not need to continue.

In early December, my dad was admitted back into the Civic Hospital himself as an inpatient to await a second surgical procedure to repair the dura. The dura is a three-layer thick sheath around the brain, just beneath the skull. His dura, likely due to the radiation treatments, had not been able to heal properly and therefore cerebral spinal fluid had been leaking out of his skull and pooling into a baseball size bubble over his right temple. It was horrifying to see. It stretched the skin of his eye, slightly altering his beautiful, warm face. He needed to come back to the hospital every second day to have it drained, only to have it fill back up again within forty-eight short hours.

Finally, he was going to get this fixed. Two days after he was admitted, my mom was moved to her continuing care hospital in the city, luckily, not too far from the Civic. The move there was surreal, and I remember entering that hospital my arms draped with my mom's coat, my shoulders heavy with her bags, and all my organs in my throat as I knew that this would be the last place I would ever come to see or care for her again.

After Sheila got the update from my stepdad that my mom had been moved to this facility and that the diagnosis was likely now palliative, she sent me a message blaming me for having allowed her to have finished the radiation and therefore killing her. She told me that I should have left her well enough alone. "Hadn't she suffered enough?" Then, for good measure, she threw in a comment about a post and picture about my dad commenting that it was nice to see that I apparently had more respect for my dad than I did for my mom because I at least posted a nice picture of him smiling. Too bad I could not have given her the same respect.

I am telling you now that these comments did not roll off my shoulders the way you might think they did. That one stung deep. I cried myself to sleep on what was already a day so overly emotional and scary – seeing two parents between three different hospitals; knowing that my mom's would be her final stop on this earth; learning to accept the word "palliative" and pivot my thinking from *she may come home* to *how do I tell her she is not coming home?* to *how do I make the best of this now for her going forward?*

Sheila's comments had me cowering in my bed wondering if I had any clue what I was doing. They had me wondering if I had dishonoured my parents, if everyone else saw me the same way Sheila did. I had to dig deep to pull myself back out of that mindset and put my two feet on the floor the next morning.

WORDS TO LIVE BY

I had the incredible pleasure of seeing Maria Shriver speak once and of all the amazingly empowered things she said, and there were lots of them, there was one that I walked away with that held more power than the rest. It was a three-sentence motto that she tells her kids often and one that used to elevate me through the darkest times: "Head up. Shoulders back. Walk forward."

And that was it. I would have to walk forward without Sheila's opinions dragging behind me. A reminder of these words gave me the strength to keep walking forward despite the people who were trying to drag me down.

These may not be your words. Those three little sentences may not speak to you at all. But find the ones that do. Write them down. Repeat them to yourself out loud. Do it again. And again. Live by them.

You must create your healing environment. Nobody else is going to do it for you. You choose who gets to be in it and who does not. Who is guiding you forward and holding out a hand for support? Who is getting in the way making you look backwards?

Lose the joy suckers and the energy wasters and choose to surround yourself with the army of angels that is desperately waiting to help you. Let the love in.

8

LOSE THE FEAR

I had no clue what to do. When I arrived up to her new room in her new and dismal hospital she looked almost as if she were already gone. It was December 4. She was finally being moved to her new home at St. Vincent's, a continuing care hospital. I am not sure that the off-putting dismal feeling of the hospital came from its murky, faded, yellow walls or if it were the odd turquoise coloured trim and doors, or if it were the fact that this would be her final home. Regardless, who picks these paint colours? The hallways reeked of human feces and antiseptic wipes. It was far grimmer than the acute care hospital she had just come from (the same one that my dad was now back in).

I cautiously walked into her room, not knowing what to expect. The gurney she had been wheeled in on still sat parked beside her hospital bed. I could only see the gurney from the back. It appeared empty. I expected to come around to the front end of the parallel beds and see her propped up and cozy in the proper hospital one but when I came around front, it was empty. I then noticed that I had walked right past her. She was there, still in the gurney, slumped completely to one side with an arm stuck through the side rail all the way up to her shoulder. Her right cheek was pressed against the cold metal bars. She was somewhere between asleep and awake.

She had become so limp, so weak. She did not even use her voice as much as to ask for help or verbalize any discomfort. It was as if she was not even aware at first of the awkwardness of her body position. I asked her if she was okay, and she managed a grunt. She had arrived there easily twenty minutes before I had. Had they just left her like this all this time?

I waited but no one came. I was too afraid to attempt moving her myself after the spaghetti noodle awkwardness that caused me to call an ambulance in the first place two weeks earlier.

The pain set in as her arm hung there pathetically and I finally rang her emergency call bell for some help. No one came. She had cried out in pain, begging me to help her with her arm but I had no clue what to do with her deadweight body. Helping her stand up from the couch while lowering my center of gravity and taking a wide stance and supporting her properly at the elbow was one thing but to lean over bed rails and heave a 185-pound woman up and over an entire one-foot distance with no help at all would be risking my physical health and compromising my ability to ever help her again. Not because I was weak, but because I was not trained.

We waited for more than forty minutes for someone to come in. To this day I am not sure why they wheeled her in and left her there with no one coming to transfer her or even check on her. I already hated this hospital.

Each day things seemed to get worse, both for my mom and for my faith in this place's ability to care for her. I wondered if Sheila had been right. Should I have just let her go sooner? Had I made the right call? Was this the best place for her? I wished so much that I had been forced to make that decision on my own.

She needed to be rotated every two hours not to develop bedsores. (This is standard, so if you have a parent who is not being moved this often, brush up on your core strength now.) We would go hours without anyone ever coming in, let alone coming in heaving her body around. Within one week she had developed a bedsore. I was growing furious and decided to start researching and learning the techniques for physical care on my own. If I stayed in the fear of hurting her or feeding her incorrectly or doing something wrong because I did not understand enough about the disease, then I was not giving her the care she needed from me and was not able to be the daughter that I wanted to be.

I signed up for any free online training that I could. I watched every video. I asked the staff – on the occasions that I did see one, which, I am happy to say got a lot better as the weeks went on – every question I could think of. I probably drove them nuts with my nonstop questioning on everything they did, not because I was questioning their abilities but because I had developed a desperate thirst for knowledge around care practices and glioblastoma. I had joined online and in-person support groups (before the pandemic, of course) and took more notes than I did in all high school and college combined. If my parents needed a full-time expert, I was hell-bent on becoming one.

I needed to know that if she slumped half off her bed, I would not be at the mercy of an overworked nurse on a lunch break to help her back into a safe and comfortable position. I insisted on feeding her myself, which meant encouraging her to feed herself but monitoring her, instead of having the hospital staff feed her too quickly because they had too many other patients to get to and then leave me standing in front of her holding the big steel bowl as she vomited it all back up ten minutes later because they had forced her to eat it too quickly. I had done that enough times.

I took a hospital training on feeding patients and decided that eating would be an experience for her that I could still create joy and calmness in. She had already lost her ability to walk and had been catheterized and in adult diapers for weeks. Neither of those things was going to change. Eating could still be savoured together.

I started a new workout routine in my basement with lots of core strength and heavy lifting to ensure my body could withstand the hourly rotating of my mom and guiding my dad with my stability as I would take him on walks through his hospital hallways after his second surgery.

It was mid-December and I still had two parents in two separate hospitals. I had settled into more of a routine. I would spend my mornings getting the kids ready for school, packing my snacks and lunch for the day, dropping them off and then heading to my mom. I would stay to care for my from breakfast through to her lunch, help her feed herself both as best I could, wheel her to her physio in the afternoons, encourage her through it while I wondered if she wanted to punch me in the face; physio was not her favourite and she was only mildly amused at me sitting in front of her full of team spirit shouting, "Yes, Mom. That was amazing. You can do it." I would then wheel her back to her room and tuck her back into her bed for a nap and then head to the Civic to spend the afternoon with my dad. Jackie would either stay and enjoy an extra bit of company or she would duck out for an hour or two and head home to do some laundry, shower or tidy up their house. I loved those afternoons with my dad. He would keep me laughing the whole time, even with drainage tubes coming out of his neck or spine.

Then I would get back across the city, pick up the kids from school, settle them at home, make dinner, wash lunch containers, break up fights, kiss scraped knees or banged heads, give baths, read books, go do a short workout in our basement gym, talk to my husband for 4.3 minutes about our days, wonder how we were going to keep going on like this, pass out, wake up, do it all over again. Every couple of days the schedule could have been punctuated with crying breakdowns.

That lifestyle is crazy. It is not for the faint of heart. And you are already doing it, so you already know. And if you are reading this as a possible preparation for what you might someday need to do, you have been warned. But you do have the strength inside you. I do not mean the strength to squat 200 pounds or bicep curl like a beast but the strength to lose the fear of stepping up and becoming their voice, their eyes, and their muscles.

Do not let the fear of hurting them or doing the wrong thing prevent you from bonding with them. Learn what you need to learn to be qualified enough to do it with confidence. Know that they would much rather want you to care for them and help them than a stranger with cold, latex-gloved hands. Know that the experts are there for you to learn from. Ask them questions. Be curious. No, you are not bothering them. And if you are, that is okay.

Most people go into a profession because they love that topic. Teachers become teachers because they love to teach. Math majors choose math because, guess what, they *love* math. (Weird, right?) Nurses and doctors chose medicine because it genuinely fascinates them, and we all love to talk about the things that fascinate us. Ask them the questions you want the answers to. Chances are they will be forever grateful to have a capable family member there that they know can competently feed their patient and lighten their load so that they can run to their next patient.

It turned out that the nursing and support staff at St. Vincent's hospital were not utterly incompetent. They were tragically spread thin, and the patients were paying the price. Sadly, this is the reality in most Canadian hospitals today, and is now made worse with COVID-19. Not enough workers, too many patients. As caregivers, we need to step up and support our family members where the system has otherwise fallen short and failed them.

My mom could barely lift her hand to her face to scratch her nose. She did not need me walking into her hospital room each day all small and mousy and acting like a weenie. (I chose this word partly because it paints the picture but more honestly because it makes me giggle like a twelve-year-old.) She needed me to pull myself up by the bootstraps and get to work.

Much of this goes back to playing the part. You are now an unpaid personal support worker. Congrats. You may be wiping bums, changing briefs, rotating your parent, feeding them, assisting with a lift if they require one. You are going to see things you did not want to see and hear things you did not want to hear. This is the time to stop being uncomfortable about it and step up into this role for them.

You can use this power to not only become a team player in their care but an advocate for them when they can no longer advocate for themselves. And if they are staring down the face of brain cancer, or any other destructive disease, they will eventually need your voice.

Social media post from May 29, 2020:

"I will preface with this: on an individual level, 95 percent of the nurses we have encountered over our hospital-filled journeys have been nothing but compassionate, competent, and caring. As a collective, however, an alarmingly large shortage in staffing has led to way too many downfalls in health care. I am going to paint a picture that may be uncomfortable to read.

"I arrived at my mom's hospital one morning and discovered that she had dried vomit caked into her neck. Her hair was crusted with it. Her left shoulder had, at one time, been soaked in it and had now also dried up leaving her gown stiff, flakes of dried regurgitated food falling off and creating a pile in her bed underneath her left side. When the nurse walked in with her breakfast tray, I asked at what time she had been sick throughout the night and the nurse informed me that she hadn't. I pointed to her shoulder and said, 'Well, she is covered in it, and it's all dried up now so it can't have been that recent. I am just wondering why nobody has changed her or cleaned her up?' The nurse responded with, 'Let me get her chart and check.' She then came right back with her file, looked up at me, and honest to goodness said, 'Nope. The night nurse didn't report any vomiting. I guess she wasn't sick.'

"I wasn't sure if laughing or crying were the most suitable option. I settled on disbelief and just stared at her, speechless. I, again, pointed at her and said, 'Well, no matter what the chart says, she did vomit because it's all over her and smells. I know that you have other patients to get to and feed, but can we change her gown at least please?'

"The nurse, as she gently rolled the side tray closer to set up in front of my mom, replied, 'I will just go feed my other patients first and then I will change her after that so go ahead and feed her breakfast first. I will be about an hour and a half.'

"The laughing and crying threatened to arrive at the same

time again. I chose this time to take a deep breath and avoid either. I politely answered with, 'No. I am not going to have my mom eat while she is covered in her puke. I understand that you have other patients that need you and so yes, a bath and full cleanup can wait, but I would like you to, at the least, take a few minutes and help me change her gown. Would you let your mother eat coated in her barf?'"

I could have called this an isolated incident except that I have many of them. I have many from each hospital that my parents have been at. If you are not there, who is doing these things for them? Who is putting their foot down for them? Who has their best interest in mind because nobody loves them like you do? It cannot be the nurses because they have other patients to feed. They need to feed and medicate so many other people besides your parent. If that is true, who other than your parent's own partner or children is putting them first?

There are different foundations for every disease imaginable that offer free webinars loaded with great information. Use the resources you have at your fingertips and educate yourself and others around you. You will be able to serve your parent, yourself, and so many other people down the road in such a big way. You have been given a job offering that probably thought you were not ready for. I didn't' think I could wipe my mom's nose let alone change her diaper. I pretended that was my job and that there was no other option. I trained for the position with education and physical fitness so that I could do the best possible job of it and so that my mom would never get stuck, crying out in pain, in the bed rails again.

SHOWING UP

How do you truly show up for someone who is dying? There are going to be times when you need to man up and take their gown off to replace it with a clean one because they just accidentally knocked their water all over themselves and no one's coming even though you have rung that damn bell so many times. I get it, you were not prepared to see your parent naked. Neither was I. But then I did it once and stopped caring and it became weird never again. Now, I am mindful that in many cultures this carries a heavier weight than in others and in some, none.

My mom's side of the family is French Catholic so nudity was not a thing they did. They covered up. My dad's side – slightly more liberal – did not care so much. I was born and raised somewhere in the middle which basically meant that I was naked all the time and they never were. Some of these showing up moments are going to require physical strain, some are going to require mental preparedness, and some are just going to be plain awkward.

While I loved the showing up aspect of getting right to business and gloving up to give my mom a bed bath or help her into her lift, or take my dad for another slow, laboured, wobbly walk around the hallway, my favourite showing up moments were the ones where I just had to "be." And let me tell you, those are the richest, the deepest, the most beautiful. But can be the absolute hardest.

Social media post from March 17, 2020:

"She sleeps a lot more now. And she talks a lot less. The days are getting harder, and we are constantly being reminded that the end is coming nearer.

"Today I brought her to physio and squatted down beside her wheelchair as we waited for the physiotherapist to come and get her. My arms leaned on her armrest. I stay mostly on her right side now. Her head only and always goes to the right side as keeping it upright is something she has grown too weak to do. I stared up at her and she stared down at me. Her eyes never left my face other than to study its perimeter. She seemed to be taking in every scar, every freckle, every curve.

"I then quietly asked her, 'What are you thinking about, Mom? Or are you just happily staring at my beautiful face?' with a hint of sarcasm. She just smiled at me and nodded.

"And I wondered in that moment what she must be thinking. What is she thinking when she looks at me this way and doesn't look away? What must she think of all this mess that our life has become? How different from the looks she gave me as a baby, or as a tantrum-throwing child and then as a sassy preteen and into a defiant teenager. There were certain looks that accompanied each struggle we caused each other and for each we faced together. I remember the look she gave me when I told her I was getting married. The look on her face as she delivered the most beautiful speech at our wedding. The look when we told her she would first be a grandparent. And then again. And again.

"The looks continued and varied and always etched in my memory. But none like the way she looks at me now. There is a stillness. A calm. Something that I hadn't seen before. I will always wonder now, as she no longer has the words, what she is thinking as she studies my face. And for now, I will wonder how many days I will have to watch her do so. Or worse, were these looks always there, and I was just too busy to notice?"

Don't be so busy now that you miss these moments.

In the quiet is where we feel our deepest feelings and so, the quiet can be scary. do you remember when you were a little kid and you got sick? You would typically have to spend the day in bed or flat out on the couch. Do you remember that the one thing you wanted most was the comforting proximity of your mom or dad? The warmth of their touch. If you are reading this book, I assume you have been honoured with the absolute blessing of caring for your mom or your dad at the end of their life and therefore I pray that you were also blessed with a mom or dad that cared for you through the beginning of yours.

I remember the serenity, of having either of them just come and sit on the edge of my bed or the couch. I would relent in the feeling of the mattress compressing down with their weight and my body would roll closer to them with the pull of gravity. It was instant comfort, just knowing that they were there. They did not even need to be singing or reading to me or telling me stories, they just needed to be close. That was enough.

If you are reading this as a parent, especially a mom, you know that kids have this innate need to be around you all the time. If you pee, they show up outside the bathroom door before your butt has hit the seat. If you sneak away up the stairs to your room to make a phone call or grab something off your bedside table or breathe, they are calling your name before you have crossed the threshold. Your parents, sick and vulnerable, now need you to just be there, close to them. Imagine how comforting it would be for a parent knowing that they had raised a child that not only loves them enough to go through vulnerable and uncomfortable things for them, but also enough to give them their time to just be there beside them.

That, to me, is what dignity is. It is not lipstick or a comb. It has nothing to do with how much hair your parent is losing or who sees it. You can honour your parent's dignity by doing the dignified thing yourself. You can honour their dignity by being brave enough to not only embrace it yourself but to show the world what the beautiful side of dying can look like. You can honour their dignity by showing up for them in every possible way, quiet or loud, comfortable or uncomfortable, pretty or not pretty. Dignity is love and love is unconditional.

Drink the water, eat the food, move your body, get supportive shoes, buy a calendar, lose the baggage, educate yourself, and train appropriately. Because if not you, then who?

9

THE SELF-CARE MYTH

Here is a line you are going to hear often: "Make sure you take time for you."

Again, like the articles coming your way, it is well-intended. It is delivered with so much love and devotion, but it might make you want to drop kick each person who says it over the neighbor's hedge. Why? Because you cannot possibly fathom adding one more thing to your list.

The term "self-care" was coined back in the fifties encouraging recovering hospital patients to focus on physical and personal hygienic care to gain independence throughout recovery. It then morphed into something that has become seemingly unattainable for so many of us, especially busy moms, caregivers, and anybody else who does not have an expendable cash flow. Often, when we think of self-care, we think of spa days, mini-vacations, or even just long hot bubble baths. I believe our brains go there because so often the messages we get encouraging self-care are going to look something like this: "Hey Laura, just wanted to check in on you. I am sorry to hear about your mom and your dad. What are the odds of both at the same time? I have been following along with your updates and wanted to say how strong you are. *Please* make sure you are taking time for yourself every day though too. Maybe you should book a massage or head to Le Nordik for the day."

If you are committing yourself to helping someone live out their days with dignity, grace, and joy, you are already getting those things in return. You are likely not going to want to take a day away from your parent when you are not sure how many days you will have left with them.

Sure, self-care can certainly be days spent at Scandinavian spas. Who would not want that? But where you are now may not be focusing on day-long retreats with girlfriends. And while we both know that there should be zero guilt around taking an hour or so to book yourself a glorious massage, you may not be prioritizing that (only dreaming about it) as part of your self-care practices.

YOU ARE DOING BETTER THAN YOU THINK

Let us talk about what realistic self-care can look like for you. I sat with my therapist one day and told her that I was stressed out about self-care. I recognized that it was an oxymoron the second it left my mouth. She just looked at me with a puzzled expression, tilted her head to the side, and said, "Hmm" as therapists so often do.

I explained to her that there was so much pressure from everyone to make sure I was taking time for myself but how on earth was I supposed to take time for myself when I spent every day running from school to hospital to school to home to kids sports to back home again? Where does a manicure fit into a full-time caregiving life with a parent who is not allowed to be left alone due to risk of seizure. Or, when I am splitting my days between two hospitals across the city from my home. It was starting to feel like this whole "self-care" thing was just another thing I needed to add to my schedule, and I was so overwhelmed by it.

She then asked me what my favourite part of my day had been thus far. I answered with the twenty-minute drive from the school to the hospital. It was always quiet. (At that point my mom was already full-time in the hospital and no longer living with me.) I would drop the kids off, kiss them all good-bye, get myself a fresh coffee and listen to music for the entire twenty glorious, uninterrupted minutes before park-ing, taking ten deep breaths, getting my lunch bag, and steadying myself for another day of hospital life and another thrilling and gut-wrenching game of "What will I see when I walk into her room?" But that short twenty-minute drive with the sun and the hot coffee and whatever was on the radio – it was a teensy piece of quiet heaven.

My therapist gently said, "Well then, Laura, that *is* your self-care. And maybe at this place in your life, that is all that you are going to be able to hold on to." And just like that, I realized I had a self-care routine. It was not glamorous, it did not smell like lavender or include anyone squeezing different parts of my body until they hurt, but it was mine. From then on, instead of driving to the hospitals in the morning with anxiety or fear while I stressed about the day's events and schedule, I drove more slowly, cranking the radio louder, basking in my bubble on wheels of quiet solitude. My car became my soft place to fall. Self-care became a whole lot easier.

Get a piece of paper and a pen. Make a list of all the things you may already be doing that are self-care for you right now. I know that you are drinking water. That is one. You are eating the rainbow. That is two. You are already doing better than you think. Take a second and bask in that. But then try to come up with a few that we have not outlined as steps for not falling apart in this book already.

Do you have dance parties in the kitchen while you pack your lunches for the day? Do you have a quiet drive to the hospital or parent's house? Do you sit by them and read a great book while they sleep? Do you take moments to connect with them, reminisce, share memories? Do you eat at your kitchen table as a family without screens? These are all small ways we are already taking care of ourselves and nurturing our souls without even realizing or planning it.

MEDITATION

For years I have felt this pressure to learn how to meditate properly. I have a busy brain. I am not a calm person who can zone out the way that my husband has mastered. When we sit to watch a movie together, he will pay attention in a way that makes me believe he has superpowers that he is not letting on to. I, on the other hand, will plan an entire fundraising event in my mind, write a grocery list to photographic memory and wonder what life would be like if we had a fourth baby, all while turning to him every four minutes to ask him things like, "Who is that guy?" "What just happened there?" "What the heck is Hydra?" (We watch a lot of Marvel.) I drive him completely nuts. I did the same thing to my dad and brother growing up and drove them nuts, too.

I always pictured myself to be not the meditative type. I have played hockey all my life. I like to get my aggression out through physicality, not mindfulness. I had let myself off the hook from this whole idea of being still until curiosity built and finally, I had to give this thing a try.

I was the worst. My predictions were right. It was never quiet in this head of mine. I would plan and plot and analyze and sing songs and before I knew it my toes were tapping and my fingers twitching to beats that were repeating in my head on shuffle. This stuff takes practice. I knew it was not something that was going to come easy for me and did not feel like I had the time to start practicing when I was implanted deeply in the throes of full caregiver life. But that was when I knew I needed it the most. The irony is cruel.

I spoke to a friend one day who opened my eyes to something new and oh so liberating. Now, a true spiritual practice is one thing and needs to be done passionately and with a disciplined commitment. But a meditation of the mind, a stillness, a calm, an intense focus, can be obtained in so many other ways than sitting cross-legged on a folded towel in your walk-in closet with a battery-operated tea light candle in front of you.

I am a horticulturist by trade and while I had temporarily handed off my business to my staff, I still loved nothing more than to get into my garden on the days that I could. (Also, I am in Canada so more accurately on the days that I could in the months that would allow it.) One of my favourite ways to spend time with the kids after a long hospital day and a school pick-up was to putter around in the garden next to them while they practiced bike riding or back handsprings on the lawn. This *was* a form of meditation, and therefore self-care.

According to my dear friend, who is sort of the expert in all things meditation, when you are gardening, you are literally working with your hands in the earth. You are connected to a higher spirit/ source. Also, soil is a proven anti-depressant. Get in it. Get yourself into the garden. If you do not have one, create a small one or start with a few potted plants. Gardening, plants, and soil also raise your frequency.

If you live in the northern climate like me and endure long stretches of winter with much less outdoor time, get yourself some indoor plants. My self-care and meditation would often happen on Sunday mornings while I walked around my house with my coffee in one hand, watering can in the other, tending to my plants. They will not only purify your air but also add extra humidity to the air as well during those dry winter months. Plus, plants on their own vibrate at a high frequency and therefore they automatically raise yours. You do not even have to be outside.

When we work with nature, we are so connected to source that we are automatically in a state of calm and meditation. The act of focusing on the plant itself or the gardening task at hand brings us even deeper into meditation as well.

The same can be said for something as mindless as doing the dishes. If your focus is going to one thing while you quietly and methodically work with your hands, you are in a state of meditation. Are you a crafter? A sewer? A carpenter? All these activities require focus, pulling your thoughts and attention into the present moment and allow you to zone fully into a state of directed concentration without conscious thought.

If none of these things resonate or work with your life, and meditation is something that intimidates you, whether it be for the time commitment or the stillness, try a guided meditation app while you fall asleep at night. Or use your falling asleep time to focus on your body, your breathing, the feelings from the top of your head, all the way down to your toes. Focus on one body part at a time and breathe deeply into it, imaging all that breath going straight to that part, filling it up with blood and oxygen, and releasing it.

Do not let yourself skip meditation or calmness just because you are not on a mountain top in Bali. Recognize the feeling of pure love and connection when they come up, close your eyes, breathe it in and there you go, you are meditating.

RAISE YOUR FREQUENCY

I wonder now if I had understood this then if my teenage years would have had me walking less slouched, less hair hiding my face, less mumbling and so much less mopiness. But then again, maybe that's the teen's rite of passage. We are made up of energy and molecules that are continuously vibrating at a frequency that is ever changing. Our frequency is affected by our thoughts, what we eat, what we do, and who we are around.

On the days when you are feeling lower than low, you are vibrating at a low frequency. On the days where you are considering running for Prime Minister, you are vibrating at a high frequency. Most days fall somewhere in between. But there are things we can do to raise our frequency right away when we feel ourselves slipping down into that mopey, feet dragging, teenage angst version of ourselves. Here are a few quick go-tos.

Water

Water raises your frequency. I cannot say enough about water. Drink the damn water. Pause here and go refill your bottle.

High-Frequency Food

Here is a hint – it does not come in packages and spans every colour of the rainbow. If you have been paying attention, you are already doing this. Eat from the earth.

Epsom Salt Baths

Yes, we have established that marathon long Epsom salt bubble baths with the lavender dead sea scrolls and floating hibiscus petals may not be happening for you right now (how great does that sound though?) but if you can, find the time once or twice a week to submerge yourself into a soaker tub of skin-tingling hot water with Epsom salts (which you can buy at your local dollar store), even if only for 20 minutes. Let the hot water envelop you in a comforting hug. Let the Epsom salts slough away the day's stresses and raise your vibration. Feel better, sleep better, you deserve it.

Exercise

Automatic game changer. I have never in my life found anything that makes me feel more alive, more energetic, more vibrant, and even more sexy (yes, covered in sweat, smelling like a locker room, cheeks flushed, exercise has magic powers) than when I get off the ice, the soccer field, or finish a hard workout. It does not have to be to this intensity though if you are wondering if I am seriously suggesting you lace up skates and find a frozen pond. Go for a walk in your neighborhood. Have a dance party in the living room. Make an obstacle race for kids or grandkids in the yard and do it with them. Want to send your frequency to new heights? Get moving.

Music

Automatic fun maker, if you choose the right music of course. If it is going to induce a tidal wave of tears, maybe save that one for another time. (More on feeling your feelings in the next chapter.) Throw on your favourite and most inspiring tunes. Make yourself a "raise your frequency" playlist.

Nature

Enough said. You get it. Sun, sand, soil, or surf. All four together or each on their own are a recipe for high vibes. Add a plant. Hug a tree. You are feeling better just thinking about it, aren't you?

The key here is to keep good habits. If you have already implemented some of these things into your life based on what we have talked about in previous chapters, then you are already doing more self-care than you realize. My friend Anuschka, a glioblastoma thriver herself, teaches cancer patients how to raise their frequencies to help heal and encourages everyone to write a "Raise Your Frequency" list for themselves. Mine would certainly include gardening, hockey, and baths but yours might include sunset walks, reading, lying naked in your backyard. We are not here to judge, but to encourage a list that will work for you.

LAUGH

Really, this could have gone in the raise your frequency list above, but I felt it deserved its own category down here because so many of us forget how to do this in hard times. When we are faced with mortality of a parent, especially if that parent is still young, we feel that their suffering must mean our suffering. We can get sucked into the idea that we cannot laugh in such a horrible time, or it would mean we are being disrespectful. This can get much worse for anyone who is sitting in grief and loss as well. So, let's talk it out now and avoid it snowballing into a feeling of you having to hole yourself up into bed with the curtains closed, but you'll have those days too, waiting for all grief to pass before you let yourself laugh again. Because, and I hate to say this, the grief is not passing. Not ever.

You will quickly learn that joy does not need to come from money or grand gestures and that while facing an unprecedented diagnosis you can still laugh all day, every day. You can laugh at your situation, you can laugh at each other, and you can laugh at yourselves. And when you get tired of that, you can yell and scream and cry and feel the hurt all the way down to your toes.

Laugh now. Laugh while they are still here. Laugh with them. Wouldn't that be exactly what they would want to see from you? Fun can be had right until the end. That does not mean that fun will replace sorrow and you will not be feeling the hard feelings and sadness around this reality, but they can coexist beautifully. You just need to make space for both.

My dad taught us this early with his signature sense of humour. My brother, an exact comedic replica of him, has kept me laughing the whole way through the journey of loving our parents until they were gone. The jokes from our dad started immediately about how he only had half a brain. Whether it was jokes about the zipper he referred to that snaked around the right side of his skull (his forty-two staples), or the spaghetti junction of drainage tubes protruding from his body, or the smushy grapefruit-sized bubble he walked around with for two months above his right temple from the leaking cerebral spinal fluid, he was always making a joke about something, always smiling, always keeping us all in stitches (he would have made a bad dad joke here too.)

He could look at us in one moment and tell us that he would miss us when he was gone or to take care of each other and his grandkids, have us all in tears, and then make a joke about that leaving us in a confused state of hysterics walking a tight rope between full-blown laughter and full-blown breakdown. Richard has the same innate gift, and it keeps me sane when I am close to teetering off the tight rope in the wrong direction.

When Richard's birthday came around on January 9, 2020, my dad had already been home recovering from dura surgery for several weeks and our mom was continuing to decline fast in her new hospital. We had scheduled a meeting that evening with her doctor and the social worker to meet with me, Rich, and Marc, to decide what measures we would take for her going forward. On Richard's birthday we sat around a conference table and made the official decision that she was chronically palliative. It was emotionally heavy. There were tears from all of us.

We then went back to her room and carried on with life and her care. Would we bother telling her? She still thought she would be coming home and would ask us most days if we thought she could come home that weekend to sit on her porch and enjoy a glass of wine. We had only just confirmed in that meeting what we already had known to be true for over a month now, she was never coming home. We chose not to tell her and to just keep focusing on making everything joyful for her.

I knew Richard's birthday was probably not looking the way he would have liked it to. I snuck down to the hospital's store, purchased a bag of two-bite® Brownies, found a birthday candle app on my phone, and proceeded to stack the brownies up in a cake-shaped pile, held the phone above them, and we all sang Happy Birthday. Even a few people from down the hall joined in. He blew on my phone to extinguish the electronic candles, I handed him a beer I had smuggled in, and we had a great time and tons of laughs. Then I went back home and cried my face off.

It's not about pretending the hard feelings are not there and don't exist. They do. But they can be honoured and felt when they come up and when they do not, choose joy. Choose laughter. It is okay to feel both without one taking away from the other. Care for yourself enough to make room for laughter.

ONE MINUTE AT A TIME

I was so overwhelmed after my mom's original diagnosis. My friend Theresa had reached out to me to see if I was okay and I responded with, "Just trying to take it one day at a time." She offered back words that changed the way I would enter each day after that, and I will be forever grateful to her for that. She simply said, "No. One minute at a time."

When you are in the eye of the storm and just trying to survive, an entire day can seem insurmountable. You cannot focus on being happy for the day or getting through the day or even planning for the day because you truly may not have any clue what that day might hold. Break it down even smaller. Some days you may need to go minute by minute, moment by moment. Give yourself room to be flexible. Do not over-commit yourself to extracurriculars or too many appointments. Hospital life is tumultuous and unpredictable. Leave room for pivoting if suddenly a new symptom, or event, or diagnosis comes up that no one had expected.

Focus on surviving in each minute or task and thriving in the ones where you can. Love yourself enough to realize that you are stronger than you think, or you would not have been the one called on to do this work.

Celebrate that strength and commitment you have given your parent with self-care practices that are small and realistic. Someday you will get to the spa and your nails will be perfect and your lashes done, if that is your mojo. But until then, breathe in those car rides, feel the music in your soul, dance around the kitchen naked one minute, and let yourself cry the next. And then, get back up, drink a glass of water, and give yourself a hug. That is self-love.

10

DIG DEEP

As I write this chapter, I am held up in a hotel room in the exact city I live in. We are in the midst of a global pandemic. If you are reading this book, you have either lived through it or heard your parents talk about it endlessly. I wonder now what it will be called later. What will we refer to this time as?

Regardless, I am here, at the most beautiful and swanky hotel that Ottawa has to offer. Why am I here taking refuge from the people who love me unconditionally and bring me joy? I am here because this pandemic has put my city into its third wave of stay-at-home orders. Our schools have been moved to a virtual platform and that has left me with three kids homeschooling and a husband working from home at his makeshift office in our bedroom, me trying to keep two businesses afloat, grow a charity and write a book all in the confines of four walls with a small but sweet dog who barks incessantly at every passing squirrel.

This book, while serving as a guide to help you step into becoming the best caregiver you can be, is also a memoir of sorts, a forced but imperative way for me to relive the heartbreaking moments and events of the past two years of my life. And to do that in a way that would serve you as my reader and share my story in the most vulnerable way, I knew that I was going to have to dig deep. I know that you are capable of doing the same. You are capable of stopping, breathing, focusing in on your feelings, and reaching deep into the most hidden depths of your soul to pull out a strength that you have never had to reach for before.

My ability to do this started young. Since I was an athletic little girl, my dad was eager to put me in soccer and volunteer to coach. Soccer, at the time, being his favourite sport. For most of my adolescent soccer playing years, my dad was my coached me and he was undisputedly the best. He was not the most skilled soccer player, and truthfully by the time most of us made it to high school and were playing on junior or varsity teams, we had far surpassed him in not only skillsets but also in running drills and practices. My dad was different though. He did not see this shortcoming as a reason to step down and bring in someone more qualified. He saw this as an opportunity to teach these young, teenage girls to step into leadership roles. He turned the coaching ideology on its head and had *us* coach the practices and each other. He made leaders out of the whole lot of us. And we became unstoppable, winning most games by large margins and feeling limitless.

As I have mentioned, there were two things that my dad would call out to us regularly in the middle of a game. "Hustle" and "Dig Deep."

As I paralleled my soccer playing days with hockey playing days, "dig deep" became a common mantra in my life from coaches in every sport and at every level. Even when, as an adult, I started working with my personal trainer, Jason, he would often repeat those words to me and motivate me enough to execute one more squat, one more lift, thirty extra seconds holding a plank. Digging deep became something I excelled at. And it has served me well in the world of emotions now too.

The depths of feelings I would need to reach to write these words was not going to happen in a home with two frazzled adults, three stressed and bored kids and a yappy dog all piled on top of each other. I needed some space to breathe and be and feel, and so, here I am on a high-back, overstuffed armchair, feet on a matching ottoman, laptop poised on my extended legs, looking out a floor-to-ceiling window over the adjoining golf course and the Ottawa river from the twelfth floor. My parents' two candles sit on a round side table facing me. Their beautiful love and light cheering me on reminding me to dig deep. It is pretty perfect. It is the self-care getaway I needed for all the time that I was taking care of my parents but realistically would never have given myself – an entire forty-eight hours of writing. Having the ability to dig deep while caring for my mom and dad is why I am still here today and able to experience this weekend and produce this book for you. Many chapters of this book have come out of this hotel room and this is the last one I will write before I head back home to my busy family.

If you have not already concluded from the fact that I am finally taking this short time for myself, yes, my parents have both since passed. I can now enjoy the baths with the floating things and extracted salt from the sea. I can now spend the extra time with my kids without having to call for backup or worry that I forgot someone somewhere. We have not missed a birthday party, or an appointment, and my heart has palpitated far fewer times. But damn, I miss them. And damn, being an orphan, even at thirty-eight, is so, so lonely. Some days I feel like a tree without roots, worrying that if life gets too hard and I get pushed or pulled in the wrong direction, I will just topple, nothing anchoring me to the ground.

But I did get here. I did make it this far. And I know that you will too. But how do you get here ensuring that you can continue to hold your head high? How do you get through without one single regret? It may be uncomfortable but here it is. You love out loud. How do you love out loud? You say every word and ask every question and share every story. And when you are out of words or need a break, you love out loud with your presence by being there and breathing it all in, good or bad. Here is where I learned to do this.

In the stretch of November 2019 when my mom was being bounced between hospitals and one day needed a shunt and the next day did not and then two hours later did again and then that night the doctors would change their mind again, I called my friend Kyla who lives out in Calgary. She had lost her mom to breast cancer many years ago. I asked what advice she would give someone like me, knowingly about to lose a parent (in my case two) and how to do that the right way. I know that I have many lines and mottos that have stuck with me and that I have shared in this book, but she offered another one that forever changed the landscape of this experience for me, and inadvertently for so many people around me.

"Laura," she said in a steady but authoritative voice, conveying that she knew what the hell she was talking about. She had been down this road. My ears perked. "Take all the pictures and say all the things."

I immediately had a game plan. No schedule or agenda or tasks to accomplish but just exactly that. I was going to take all the pictures and say all the things and I was going to dig pretty damn deep to do it. Things were about to get a whole lot harder.

Feelings are big. They are confusing and messy and not

usually at all organized, like my thought process in starting this book. But if we try to stuff them into jars with tightly screwed-on lids, we are not only brewing a storm but cheating ourselves out of giving and receiving love to its fullest capacity. These feelings, whether light or heavy, need space to exist in order to be processed. When I suggest to people that they tell their parents how they feel about them, those people squirm and hug themselves as an intuitive form of protection.

Imagine for a moment you are the parent. Imagine that as that parent you are facing the end of your life. Imagine your child is strong and incredible enough to have opted into caring for you. The love you would know, and feel, would be incomparable. Now imagine your child looking you in the eye and telling you what they love most about you, what some of their favourite and most cherished memories with you were. Imagine they could tell you all the ways in which you have inspired them, shaped them, motivated them into becoming the incredible person that sits there today self-lessly giving you the best gift of all, their time. Imagine the feeling when they confirm for you that you are responsible for who they have become.

I thought long and hard about one thing I would want to know from my kids when I die. I would want to feel validated and recognized as a parent. What better gift than you telling them all the things they got right.

Now, I know they have likely not gotten everything right. None of us probably ever will. But at this point in their journey on earth, there is zero purpose in telling them all they have done wrong. (Unless all they have done is wronged you. Then you may need a different book.) But for the sake of focusing on the positive, sending them off with love and filling your soul back up, give them the gratitude. It may feel horribly uncomfortable, but this is your chance. And every day could be your last. Do not let it pass you by. Do not let it get to the end, leaving you wishing they had known how loved they were. Tell them now. And on the slim chance that you are reading this without even having a dying parent, tell your healthy parent all this now too.

Get as specific as you can. That whole story about how my dad teaching us to dig deep in sports taught me to dig deep in so many other areas of my life, therefore leading to so much richness in love and opportunity ... you'd better believe I told him that. What caught me most off guard was his reaction of genuine surprise.

His eyes and face lit up and he looked over at me and said, "Really?" with the warmest smile. When I nodded yes back at him and went on to elaborate, his facial expressions changed from surprise to a peaceful serenity that I cannot quite explain. It was as if I was talking directly to his soul and validating its purpose on this earth.

While my dad was alert and able to communicate for most of his time past diagnosis – a blessing I never took for granted – my mom was not as fortunate. As you know, her rapid decline had robbed her of the ability to communicate efficiently by Christmas of that year. But she could listen, so I would tell her the same stories of all the ways she rocked motherhood. My stories and thanks were never met with the same wide-eyed appreciation as my dad's reactions, making them extra hard to say, but on rare occasions she would find my eyes, linger on me for a moment and I could see it then, all the ways she wanted to say thank you. The way she would just rest her hand on top of mine over the bed rail but not say a word. Or the way she would turn her head to me and just nod faintly, all that she could manage at times, as if saying, *I heard you. I see you. I love you. Thank you.*

Meanwhile, a global pandemic went from something we had heard about overseas, to something slowly infiltrating

North America, to a sudden first case in Ottawa on March 11, 2020. The fear spread like wildfire, faster even than the virus itself, and hospitals shut their doors to visitors. While I was still allowed to be with my mom as her caregiver, nobody else was. Even Richard had been shut out. And while Jackie could be with my dad as his caregiver, nobody else was allowed and I had been shut out. I was terrified. I was terrified that I would lose him and never be able to say goodbye.

Less than three weeks earlier on the twentieth of February while Richard and I sat around our mom, feeding her lunch together, we received a text from Jackie that our dad was back at emerge because of an infection in his incision. The text was not of any urgent nature and in fact, told us not to worry, they would probably wait at emerge to be seen and then be sent home with some antibiotics. I decided to leave Rich with our mom and go to our dad and Jackie anyway. Good thing I did because he would never leave the hospital again.

He was admitted with an infection so bad that only a third surgery to remove the infected pieces of brain and skull, followed by six weeks on an antibiotic drip, were going to clear it up. I was back to being between two hospitals every day. Until, that is, COVID shut down visitation two weeks later, on March 15.

The updates on my dad had to come from texts from Jackie when she could find the time or energy. She spent every day, all day, at the hospital with him with no one to relieve or help her.

Then on March 21, a phone call came at 9:15 p.m. Kenny and I had been curled up on the couch watching a movie, kids tucked safely into their beds.

It was my dad on the other end. He had undergone surgery number four the day before. After the surgery to remove the infection, the dura began to leak again and they decided to go back in a fourth time. I was not able to see him before or after that surgery and was so grateful to hear his voice. We bantered a bit about the weirdness of the looming pandemic.

"Hey, Kid, unfortunately I am not going to survive this one."

"Dad, survive what? The cancer? You only have an infection. You are going to be home soon."

"No, Laura, not the cancer. The cancer doesn't matter anymore. They did an x-ray yesterday to figure out why I had started coughing so much and my lungs are full of blood clots. Big ones, kiddo, and a lot of them. I am not going to survive them. It might only be another day or two. I am calling to say goodbye."

"What? Dad. No. Not okay." I realized I was shaking involuntarily. I wanted to tell my pounding heart to shut up so that I could hear myself think. I needed to stop the noise. This did not make any sense. What was he saying? How could he be talking about blood clots? He had cancer. He was going home soon. But he was dead serious. His lungs were full of them. We had guessed that his throat clearing, and strained voice was from him being so run down from two surgeries in nearly as many weeks. We could not have guessed this.

I went silent.

"I am calling to say goodbye, Kiddo." He repeated.

"No. Dad, no. You can't. I can't. I can't say goodbye. I am not ready to say goodbye. I want to give you a hug. How can I say goodbye like this?" Nothing I was saying at that point was audible.

My dying dad tried his best to help calm me down. He told me it would be okay. He told me that Rich and I would have to take care of each other as our mom was soon going to be gone too. He told me to keep taking care of her while I could. He told me, over a phone call, how proud he was of both of us, of Kenny, of the precious grandchildren I had given him. He asked me to say goodbye to each of them and tell them all how loved they are by him.

I wailed no into his ear at least twenty-nine times before calming down only slightly, enough to accept that this was it. This would be our goodbye. I tried to listen. I chewed my fist in order to stifle cries and not wake the kids while I obediently coughed out shaky little, "okays" to everything he said.

And then I tried to hang up. I couldn't. He couldn't. "Goodbye, Laura. I love you so much. Don't forget that, okay?"

"Dad, thank you for everything you did for me. Thank you for teaching me to be strong. I hate this, Dad. I can't hang up. "

"I know. I'm so proud of you. I want you to always know how proud of you I am. I can't hang up either. This is so hard. But I love you so much. I don't want to hang up, but I have to, okay? I have to call your brother to say goodbye to him too." My heart shattered further at the thought of my little brother experiencing exactly this feeling and me not being able to protect him.

After a long-drawn-out goodbye, we hung up. Hanging up had never felt so painful. I sat and shook until I fell over onto Kenny, who had been sitting perfectly still and listening on the couch beside me with a hand on my back. I cried into his chest with my fist still planted in my mouth. I realized in doing so why my daughter does this during anxiety attacks. There was something comforting there. Something Freudian, maybe. Whatever. It helped.

I did not go to sleep after that – understandably. I did lie in bed and stare at the ceiling thinking of all the extra things I would want to say to him if I did get the chance to see him one last time. I was surprised that considering I had already thought I was saying all the things, my list was so long.

Unexpectedly, the following morning I received a text from Jackie that I was able to come into the hospital once this morning to say goodbye in person. Only twenty-nine minutes into my visit, a nurse showed up and informed me that I was not approved to be there. I told her I had been cleared at the main entrance, but she was hearing none of it and told me that I had to leave. I explained that my mom was also palliative with glioblastoma and that I had been cleared to see and care for her every day and that my dad's condition had unexpectedly taken a turn for the worse. I was here to say goodbye.

Her response was that I had made my case worse by letting her know that I was exposing myself at another hospital every day.

The more she spoke the hotter my face got, the more fiercely the tears pricked my eyes and the more I started shaking. Then with a blank expression, she uttered the words that cut through my soul and triggered me into a full-blown rage and panic.

"If you want to take care of your dying parents in the hospital, you are going to have to choose one."

I stared at her until she became a blur behind the falling veil of tears and through them, I yelled, "Choose between my dying mom or my dying dad? That was so unfair of you."

I ran past her crying. And there I was in the hallway, all scrunched up, wondering how a day that was already going to tear me apart could have become even more unimaginable.

I failed to understand the world we lived in. I counted thirty-one staff walking past me as I squatted there sobbing in that hallway and not one single person stopped. All too scared to get close to another human in a pandemic.

I stayed in that crouched position for an hour, my feet searing with pain, terrified that my dad's last memory with me would have been of me rushing away from his hospital bed while I tried not to throat punch the nurse as I pushed past her.

My phone buzzed with a text from my brother letting me know that he was in the lobby waiting for his turn to come up, look our dad in the eyes and say thank you for a lifetime of love. I stood slowly, wincing from the pain, then hobbled down to the lobby to let him know he was no longer allowed in. We sat together and started our long and hopeful wait for approval to get back up to him.

After four hours on hard plastic chairs, we were told to go home. His vitals had stabilized and he was no longer "imminently dying." Therefore, no visitors, not even his wife, would be allowed after today.

I went home and crawled into bed thinking there was no way I could handle any more. Then I remembered that I had no choice. My mom still needed me in a hospital bed only blocks away from my dad's and I was still permitted to care for her because of her palliative condition. And I had a lot of things to say to her now.

Do not wait until the time is right, or comfortable; tell them now. Right now. The only reason I could hang up the phone that night, as much as it hurt, was because I knew that I had already been able to say so much. I knew that he knew how much I loved him. But say it now, and again tomorrow because you never know when their situation could take an unexpected turn.

You are in a situation that many people cannot and have not had to yet understand. However, you are also in a situation that will allow you so many goodbyes, so many opportunities to share stories and laughs and find beauty and create joy together, even if you must be the one doing all the work.

Far too many people do not get that, and they are left with living in not only a world without their parent but one in which they are carrying so many what-ifs and regrets. You get the chance to not end up that same way. You get the chance to dig deep, say it all, hold your head high, and lead with your heart.

JOURNALING

There is magic that happens when we can put our thoughts onto paper. Journaling, in its traditional sense, was never something I did. I tried, at different times in my teenage years, to start a diary. I wrote about boy crushes and mean girls and embarrassing moments like when Troy Lawson put a fart bomb in my locker only to gather around with gaggle of other immature teen boys secretly watching and waiting for me to come along and fall victim to their callowness. I was left paralyzed by the smell and by the humiliation of the reactions of all the older kids walking by and taking a wide path around me as they forced chokes and cupped their hands over their faces, staring me down as I stood facing into my locker, wishing it would swallow me whole.

The challenge for me in journaling was when to stop writing. I would write and write and write until I was seven pages in and two and a half hours past my bedtime. I always felt I was doing it wrong. The thing is though, there is no such thing as journaling wrong. Whether it be a seven-page essay or three bullet points listing your feelings, it is taking the thought turmoil stirring up inside of your head and channeling it out of your body.

I had a friend in high school named Kelly. Kelly had this incredibly simple technique in her innocent sixteen years of life experience where she would 'give her problems to the wall." At night, as she laid, head spinning with concerns about school and track meets and boyfriends (we even shared one) she would put her hand on her wall and envision all her problems leaving her body through her arm, her hand, her fingertips, where the walls would hold them in place for her until morning. Her brain would immediately settle knowing that everything had a place, did not need to be sorted out just then, and she would fall asleep much easier.

I loved this concept. I tried to apply it several times but for my own brain, wired slightly differently than Kelly's, the wall was not enough. I needed to physically manifest it out of me. I continued to weave in and out of journal writing phases over the rest of my teenage and early adult years but always found myself to be much more in control of my feelings when I journaled.

One belief that has always motivated me to keep expressing myself on paper is the belief that if I could put my feelings into words then I was now in control of them, and they were not in control of me. Therefore, in my phases of falling off the journal wagon I felt so lost, overwhelmed, and confused.

I applied this belief to my journey through caregiving to have a hold and an understanding of where my feelings were coming from and to give me as much control over them as I could get. The feelings did not come easy, but they could not consume me if they could not be left to fester in my mind. The feelings of fear and shame can only exist in the dark. If we shine a light on them by bringing them into the open, then they are much easier to process and work through.

A journaling session can look many ways. I am a wordy writer, and so I will write and write and write until my eyes start to cross. If you are not a writer, start with five bullet points on the page and write an emotion or an event that caused a difficult emotion for that day, for each point. Often our biggest struggle is learning to label a feeling as opposed to just feeling yucky or irritable. If we can associate the feeling to a certain trigger or experience in the day, then we have a better and clearer opportunity to label what that feeling is or to start recognizing a pattern or experiencing that feeling each time that trigger comes up.

For example, when facing my first Christmas with two terminally ill parents and knowing that this could likely be there last Christmas, it was extremely hard for me to hear friends talk about their family traditions or, in the case of COVID, hear them complain about how their mothers weren't impressed that they weren't bringing the grandkids over for their usual Christmas dinner. People would complain to me that Christmas would not feel the same this year and a resentment would boil up inside me over the reality that for me, Christmas would never feel the same again. This had become a huge trigger for me. If I had taken those feelings of resentment and anger and envy to bed with me at night, they would have grown and grown in the warm dark space, like dangerous mold, and continued to multiply without me even realizing it. I started to write journal entries every night into an app on my phone. It became such a habit that I could not go to sleep or settle my brain until I did. It was how I unpacked every thought or traumatizing experience of every day.

Over time, I began to post many of my journal entries on social media and was able to revel in the outpouring of support that would come from people in awe of true vulnerability. The more that sort of praise came in the more I realized that expressing my inner thoughts was not only helping me, but it was also helping many other people as well.

In my public journaling I was gifted twenty-two journals. I came home several days to find gift bags of journals waiting for me at my door, stealthily dropped off by complete strangers or anonymous friends. They could also see how much my gift for journaling was helping people.

I strongly encourage you right now to pause, get a journal or even a piece of paper, and start with a bullet point list of three to five emotions that you are feeling right now. If you are a word spewing master like me, then start pouring it out. Set a timer for twenty minutes and just start writing. You may be shocked by what comes out of you. But if you are someone who does not typically share or journal and feel like you have no clue where to start, start with the trying to label three to five emotions. Then see if can attach a trigger to each one.

Magic will happen. This is a powerful tool in processing your thoughts. It will get easier if you stick with it. And then I promise you will thank me.

TAKE ALL THE PICTURES

Take the pictures. Take the pictures. Take the pictures.

I can honestly tell you that I have never thought, *Man, I wish I hadn't taken that picture of my mom.* And if I have, I was able to delete it.

But I have certainly thought, *Man, I am so glad I have this picture of my mom.* No matter what the circumstance or moment was.

Stop being weird about it. Take all the pictures.

GIVING GIFTS

What do you buy a person who is dying? This is such a strange topic due to our fear of death. But it is honestly one I struggled with entering my first Christmas with terminal parents. What do I buy them? For starters, I will likely get it back. Not to mention there is likely truly little that they need or want aside from health and time. It puts it into perspective that "things" are just that – objects.

That first Christmas I wanted my children to still be able to receive something from their Granny, but something that would be meaningful. I asked her to record (with my help) for each of the three kids a separate thirty-second message. I then took the messages, recorded on my phone, to Build-A-Bear and had a staff member there help me put them into sound clips. I made each kid a teddy bear, customizing them with what I thought my mom would have picked for each of them and had the sound clips put into the bear's paws. Now they each have a bear whose paw they can squeeze to hear a personal message from my mom to them. And yes, it still usually brings me to tears.

When my dad had originally gone in for his surgery for the first infection, weeks before the pandemic blockaded us from him, the kids had done the opposite with the Build-A-Bear idea. I had taken them to the mall and let them all design a bear for their grandpa together. Leightyn had picked a grey hoodie for the brain cancer ribbon colour. Then we did a recording of the kids saying, "We love you, Grandpa," and had that put into the bear for him. I don't think he had loved anything as much as that bear. It now lives back at our house and makes the shared custody rotation from one kid's room to the next. It also often lands itself propped up against my pillow when I am having a particularly hard day. One of the kids usually sneaks it in there for me to find as a reminder that Grandpa isn't all that far.

If you have a parent or loved one that you cannot be with as much as you would like to, here is another incredible way to make sure they always know you are thinking of them. Buy a plain white sheet or blanket, lay it out on the floor and have someone lie on top of it with their arms stretched out. Trace their arms and hands.

I did this with all three kids during the lockdown when they were missing their grandparents, and their grandparents deeply missing them, and then let them go to town decorating the blankets with fabric markers. We called them "hug blankets." These were a great way for my parents to be able to wrap themselves with the blankets and feel like their grandkids were wrapping their arms around them.

My favourite go-to gift idea, no surprise here, was a plant. I know it may seem ridiculous but go back to the frequency factor. It not only raises their frequency, but it also purifies their air. They get cleaner air, higher vibes, a living breathing thing, and a reason to smile. It is a winning combo.

Now, if you are ready and willing to get about as deep as sentimental as you have ever gone, my absolute favourite gift I ever gave my parents were letters. Luckily, I had the where-withal to do this long before they had ever gotten sick, and I am so glad I did.

In high school my friend Robin had slyly passed me a folded-up note in class. I had been having a hard time at that point in my life, dealing with my parents' unexpected divorce. Most of the notes that Robin sent me back then were those of encouragement and motivation. She had developed a mastery in that by the young age of seventeen. This note was likely no different. And probably had some stick drawing of her and me on the school's 400-meter track circle, practicing our baton hand-offs for the four-by-one relay because that is what we lived for at seventeen. Robin made sure to always remind me of the fact that sports brought me so much joy. A commonality we shared. Tucked into the note was a smaller piece of folded-up paper that displayed, in her neat, bubbly handwriting, her take on this famous quote.

"My friend, if I could give you one thing in life, it would

be the ability to see yourself through others' eyes. Only then would you realize how truly special you are."

I took that quote and kept it safely stored in my heart, always.

In my early twenties, while struggling to pay bills and thinking I had hit the jackpot when discovering I could mix my can of plain tuna with my Kraft Dinner and change lunch as I knew it, I was at a complete loss as to what to get my family for Christmas when I didn't have the money to fix my broken tooth and had been walking around looking homeless for weeks. That quote from Robyn popped back into my head one night as I struggled to fall asleep and reminded myself that just resting was beneficial and that getting back out of bed to raid the fridge was not. I reflected on what that quote meant and the tragic reality that we are always going to be our worst critics. *How did people see me?* I wondered. And thought that maybe that could be the greatest gift of all.

The next morning, I put pen to paper and wrote my parents, my stepparents, my brother and my boyfriend (now husband) a letter about how I saw them. And believe me when I tell you that despite us all being healthy, happy, humans at the time, this took some deep digging. I sobbed. I sobbed so hard with gratitude and reminders for how wonderful they each were in their way and how each of them had molded and shaped me into who I am. It was a Christmas morning that did not contain a dry eye, but a lot of full cups. Especially mine.

Over the time that my parents were sick, I decided to write them new letters. I dug deep again and scribbled out my view of them. At certain points they would be able to respond. At other times they were too sick, weak, or far gone and the letters were read by their bedside while they lied unconscious and I waited for them to stop inhaling, praying that I could at least get through the letter first. Not one of those letters was read with ease.

But there is absolute magic in knowing that they know. There is indescribable comfort in knowing that you have said all that you could say while you had the chance to say it and there is debilitating regret in knowing that you did not. dig deep down. Know that you are strong enough to rise back up if it knocks you off your feet. Love them and love yourself enough to let them know it.

11

USE THE FUEL

*"Maybe you were given this mountain so you could show others
how it can be moved."*

— RACHEL HOLLIS

W hile we learned to accept what was and
navigated the raging waters of our new lives, a
whole other tsunami was building strength on
the other side of the globe: the COVID-19 pandemic. It was
making its way across the ocean, through the skies, world
traveler by world traveler, until finally it infiltrated North
America and washed out all our lives as we knew them. I had
a mom dying in one hospital and a dad dying in another, and
neither I, nor the rest of my family, could be with either.
They were dying all alone, along with so many other millions
of scared and isolated people, none of which even had
COVID-19.

The reality was cruel and heartbreaking and enough to
make any single human want to rage against the world. I had
endured the sudden terminal diagnosis of both parents, and

now in their final year, months, weeks, days, they would lie one simple twenty-minute car ride away and I would remain stuck helplessly on the outside of the towering brick walls that confined them. I wanted to scream at every single person that ever offered the words, "it's in their own best interest," "it's for their safety," "it's to protect the other patients," or anything close to that. You cannot ever make sense of a situation like this, so do not try.

I had never felt more helpless, more victimized, more infuriated at the injustice, in my entire thirty-seven-and-a-half years. In no longer having hospitals to go to and parents that I could not care for, I found myself with a lot of extra hours to sit around and think, despite having a husband and three children. We had all, as a province, been thrust into lockdown by April and there was little else to do than sit around in a pile, confined into one house, and think about how unrecognizable and crazy our current world was. I decided that far more productive things could be done with all this time and so decided to start planning a fundraiser.

There were a few moments over the early months of 2020 where I would wake up in the middle of the night with the shocking realization that my life was happening to me. It was like a gut punch. Some nights I would shoot straight up gasping for air, mid-panic attack. Others were a far gentler rousing by the thoughts and images in my brain – a loop of the day's events, the look in my dad's eyes as I leaned over him, tucking him into a blanket while he lay on the couch in early February, looking up at me and softly saying, "Laura, we are doing this. We are winning. Every day we are winning." Because were we winning? His brain was not letting him see what we saw, that every day he was getting worse, that something seriously wrong was going on in his head, tumor or no tumor, that we had yet to discover.

These thoughts would jar me awake at night and replay

over and over. It is in the stillness, the quietest moments of the night, that you will process all that you took in that day. Your brain will protect you so that you can keep going, keep doing what you need to do: Head up. Shoulders back. Walk forward until you crash at night and all the feelings and heartache come washing over you like a tidal wave.

In so many of these middle-of-the-night episodes it would keep coming back to me, the realization that I was still standing due to the support of others. I found the will to keep going due to the musculature of the community I had built around myself. Their combined strength, through messages, cards, gifts, meals, and support, had lifted me back up when I could not do it on my own. I felt immediately blessed and empowered. As these realizations compounded over those first weeks of 2020, so did my sense of empowerment and determination to give back, pay it forward, and show all those supporters how far their hearts had reached. It did not have to stop at me.

I had realized as I shared our story publicly on social media, that more and more people would come out of the woodworks sharing their stories of losing someone to glioblastoma. These people were not strangers to me either. These were people who I had known, acquaintances, people who had left me thinking, *then why hadn't you talked about it?*

It shocked me to learn how many people seemed to be suffering in the dark when I was suffering out loud and reaping all the benefits from people and strangers alike, showing up to carry me and my family through. (Remember all that "people want to help, so let them," focus from Chapter 7?) So, if these people were not outwardly asking for support, who was supporting them? The answer is, sadly, no one. How can someone help if they do not know that help is needed?

I was spending my usual afternoon in the hospital with

my dad one day in late February, a few weeks after all the cyclical midnight epiphanies, when he gifted me with the most incredible and invaluable life lesson. Whether he knew it or not is negotiable, but I am willing to bet that his conscious brain knew something that we didn't yet. This was his time, his opportunity, to impart a little extra wisdom on me that he had amassed during his love-filled life. He made full use of it.

I had been puttering around by the window ledge, my usual assigned seat, cleaning up and arranging his finished lunch dishes onto his tray for the cafeteria staff to collect. He was rambling on, somewhat incoherently, about stuff I cannot even remember and probably did not even register at the time. I offered a bunch of well-timed uh-huhs and kept myself busy. For a while his voice had become softer and softer until nearly hitting levels of inaudible. Little did we know at the time that his lungs were quickly filling up with blood clots from the weeks that he lay there, still and straight as a board on his back, in order to not disrupt the drainage tube making an exit ramp for the cerebral spinal fluid in his brain and protruding from his spine. Then, almost completely out of the blue, something in his demeanor and his voice changed. This caveat alone caught my attention and I slowly put down all things meal-related and pulled the chair next to his bed up as close as I could get in order to hear him.

Glioblastoma can steal your thoughts and your cognitive abilities, in the same way that dementia can. One moment they are there, the next moment they are not. I arranged myself facing him, with my knees pressed hard into the plastic side rail of his hospital bed.

"Laura, I've been trying to change the world my entire life. And I did that by always putting myself in leadership positions because you can't make change from the back."

He went on to tell me that, as a child, he would always offer to take the lead on group assignments. At work, he would always offer to take the lead on projects, large or small. He had coached my soccer team so that he could teach me and sixteen other teenage girls how to be leaders and team players. He has always chosen to lead out of the knowledge that leaders create change. He believed with his whole heart that with the good of the people in this world, this world was going to be okay. And I knew that I had to be one of those good people.

Then I thought about my mom, a proper practicing Christian woman, who tithed every single week without fail. Her financial state never took away from her priority to give back. She single-handedly planned and executed a fundraiser for her church raising money to build an extension for a Sunday school for children. She collected personal care items every year to stuff into shoeboxes and sent them to less fortunate countries. After losing her own mother, whom she largely cared for in her final years, she took over caring for her older sister, no questions asked, and provided as much support for her as she possibly could. She gave so much of herself to everyone else.

Two years before their diagnosis, I had planned a large fundraising day for our local children's hospital with a group of friends. The premise was "A Day with Santa." My dad eagerly volunteered to be Santa. My mom eagerly volunteered to man the raffle table. Richard eagerly volunteered to help set up and provide relief to anyone needing breaks that day. My aunt eagerly volunteered to be Mrs. Claus. Jamie eagerly volunteered for anything and everything. My family all eagerly bought tickets, showed up, spent money, hugged Santa Claus, and helped us raise thousands of dollars in one day for our Children's Hospital.

I come from good people and therefore, I needed to keep being the good people that my parents had led me to be.

I had lost control of so much. I was losing my parents to a cancer. Its terminability was so ruthless and relentless that it would push you back on your heels causing you to play only defense, reacting to its every move instead of anticipating it. I had lost control of my businesses, handing them over to other people or putting them on a temporary shelf while I awaited glioblastoma's next move. I had lost control of my home life as a COVID lockdown held us all hostage in our homes, keeping us physically away from family, friends, and neighbours. One thing I could control was how I played the cards I was dealt, with a hand full of players I certainly never wanted. I could start a charity. I wanted no one else to suffer in the dark. I wanted to raise money for the people who were too afraid to ask for help. I wanted to raise more awareness for a cancer that was known to be the most destructive cancer in humans but that was also wildly underfunded and undereducated. I would be the voice so many people needed, offering them the support that I understood was required for them to keep their heads up, shoulders back, and walking forward. I would take back what control I could and became fiery passionate and furious about not letting glioblastoma win.

I thought of the tattoo that I ran out to get on a whim and in a state of self-indulgent fury right after my mom was diagnosed. It ran the length of my left trapezius muscle, from my neck to the top curve of my shoulder, and read in a small slight hand font, "and still I rise…" I had this moment where I pictured myself as a phoenix rising from ashes and decided that I would start using my voice for far more than just letting the world know about my parents in hopes that the emotional support I was used to getting from the two people who loved me most would now come from a pile of internet and community strangers. (And for the record, while I knew it would never be the same support, it came.)

My excitement grew at the idea that I could show all these incredible people that their acts of kindness were not in vain. My parents' suffering would not be in vain. And that the heartache, the anger, the gifts, the donations to my family, every disgusting and unforgettable moment of caring for brain incision wounds or hearing my dad's unwavering faith that he was beating cancer or watching my mom fall helplessly against my daughter's bed, they would all become fuel to build a foundation that would bring change to people's lives and to the landscape of glioblastoma as we knew it. I would not only be empowering myself but all the people that fueled me over that time too.

Right then, while listening to my dad talk about leadership, I decided to forge ahead, and start doing the work. It would be one dragon that I could slay while supporting others as they slay theirs. I decided to plan my first small fundraiser and find a fellow caregiver with a family member with glioblastoma that I could donate all the funds to. After much consideration for a world that had socially come to a screeching halt due to the pandemic, I settled on a virtual online auction at the end of March and set a goal of raising $250.

I had already connected with a girl who was living in one end of Canada while her dad was living on the other. He had been hospitalized at the Civic Hospital for nearly one year and as his only child, Chantal, would travel from Calgary to Ottawa one week out of every month to care for him. She had not worked in some time because of this, and the cost of flights was becoming a huge financial strain on her family. As someone who understood the preciousness of time with a dying parent, I knew that I had to and could help.

A donation of $250 may not provide much in the way of

contributing to flight costs but I also knew, being the recipient of so much unexpected help so many times, that a $20 bill could be enough to bring someone struggling to their knees.

I set out on my path to planning this auction with more gusto than I could have manifested in a gold medal tournament game against a rival hockey team at seventeen years old. Momentum and love fueled me. I got loud. The community rallied. And my $250 goal grew into $4,281 raised in a small, two-day, online event. Ninety percent of the work I did, I did from my phone while sitting beside my mom in her hospital bed, watching her sleep. My mind was blown, my heart was full, and my fire was ignited further. I could help people the way my dad would have wanted me to.

Social media post from March 30, 2020:

"I am tired of the feeling where I have to swallow hard to keep my breakfast down ... where my heart palpitates, and I wonder if my rib cage will even be enough to keep it from jumping out of my chest ... where my head is spinning, and nothing is in focus ... where my breaths are short and laboured and intentional because without breathing on purpose, I would probably stop altogether.

"Yet here I am again, sitting beside my mom's hospital bed as I patiently wait for her to wake enough from her Gravol-induced grogginess to eat that lunch that I have just set up in front of her. Because as I fought the urge to lose my breakfast, she was losing hers. And so, they injected her with more Gravol and she will spend yet another day sleeping and unaware.

"Despite this, my attack of anxiety and nausea didn't come from my mom. Today it came from my dad. Today we have learned that while he is already fighting to recover from two brain and one back surgery in one month, with the added immense and unexpected complications of lungs and legs full of blood clots which have landed him in the NACU, there has now been another infection found. We can't access him, not any of us. we get our updates once a day form only his wife as she is the only one allowed to call the hospital. In light of his confirmed infection this morning, the update today is another unexpected surgery to be done tomorrow. This will be his sixth surgery in seven months.

"We do not have words. We are fighting tears and fighting to breathe and fighting the urge to break down hospital doors and get to him. And soon, when I get shut out from my mom's hospital too (and it's coming) I will be fighting that urge times two.

"For right now though, I will sit here beside her for as long as I can. I will force myself to eat and to breathe. I will continue to do so until his surgery is done today, and I know he is okay. And maybe even until he can someday go home and this nightmare ends."

My dad had his surgery that day. The result was not what we had hoped and for the two days that followed he would wake up but still was not speaking. Doctors continued to assure us, over the phone, that he would bounce back.

I was spending the day taking care of my mom when the hospital chaplain walked into the room, reeking of empathy. It was now April 2. No change in my dad. I knew that the next words out of the chaplain's mouth were going to be the ones that I had known were coming but prayed I would never have to hear. "This is going to have to be your last visit today honey. I am so sorry. While your mom is palliative she isn't dying fast enough and is stable enough that we can't justify you being here anymore." That sound. It had become all too familiar. I could recognize it instantly. My heart had broken again.

I had been shut out of my dad's hospital eleven days earlier, hosted a wildly successful fundraiser four days earlier, had still not come down off the bright fluffy cloud that hovered just above the big dark ominous one that was my dad dying all alone, and now here it was, dissipating before my eyes, leaving me to fall into the darkness with a mom who would now be left to die alone too.

Leaving her that day was among one of the hardest things I had ever done. I did not rush home that day. I stayed four hours past the time I normally would have. By then schools were shut down and the kids didn't need to be picked up. Kenny's work had also become virtual, and he had been working at home for some time. I tried to breathe in every possible last in-person moment with her. I made a video to post to social media giving her a chance to say goodbye to her friends and family (take all the pictures) and giving them a chance to see her one last time, the way that she was, in the case that she may leave us during the lockdown, leaving no opportunity for any of us to ever see her again. I hugged her and wept and shook and said I loved her thirty-seven times. Each time getting weepier and weepier and trying again to not lose my breakfast as I spoke. I had had an opportunity to say a heart-splitting goodbye over the phone with my dad, now I was getting the chance in person with my mom. Somewhere around the dinner hour, as she was tiring and losing her ability to stay awake for much longer than twenty minutes at a time, I finally found the strength to steady myself and walk myself out of the hospital.

The next day, April 3, waking up to what was the first day in seven months without a hospital to go to – but with two parents in them – I received an unexpected phone call from Jackie. This was it. The infection in my dad's brain had spread too far. They just were not able to get it all with the surgery three days before. After seven weeks, four extra surgeries, there was nothing more they could do. We needed to and could come now and say goodbye. Just like that, by

4:00 p.m. that day, I was back in the car on my way to see my dad off.

He lived for nine more days. They had given us one to two in that phone call on April 3, but he took nine. Probably because he was some sort of superhero, I concluded. But in those nine days, he was unconscious. We were left with no more words, no more eye contact, no more quality of anything on his end. We knew though that he knew we were there, so we brought the quality to him. He was never alone. Richard, Jackie, and I rotated shifts so that someone was beside him twenty-four/ seven. Likely, the three of us would have packed a suitcase and set up camp right there, all together, but with visitation being shut down the rule for someone who was "imminently dying" was that there could only be one of us there at a time. My brother and I took shifts in the afternoons and overnights while Jackie took her shifts in the mornings. Richard and I shared the bedtime ritual of reading him *The Hobbit*, which he had read to us when were kids. Jackie had a steady stream of his favourite music going. But mostly we would sit, laugh, tell him jokes or funny stories about his grandkids, never letting go of his hand, and hope that we would be rewarded with the odd slight reciprocal squeeze.

For me, in most of my long hours and nights beside him, I would fill him in on fundraisers, my plan to grow my charity, to help people, to lead. I would excitedly share with him that I had aptly named the charity the Slay Society after his motivating and driving motto, "slay one dragon at a time." And then I would break down and cry, alone in my hospital chair, clad in a pale-yellow gown, soaking my gauzy disposable mask with tears, at the fact that he could never once just open his eyes, look at me and say, "I'm proud of you, Laura. You're doing it."

In the times during those nine days where I could hold

my head up and see without the blur of tears distorting my vision, I would take out my notebook and start planning my next fundraising ideas, using the image of his unconscious body, bruise splotched arms, and emerging tubes and PICC lines as further fuel. *Not in vain*, I would remind myself, *not him.*

"I won't let this all be for nothing, Dad. I promise." I would repeat over and over again as I brushed my fingers along his forehead.

I went on to plan several more fundraisers throughout the rest of that year, raising over $45,000, all going to support the caregivers who had given up their income and most of their social lives, to take care of and love someone with glioblastoma until the end of their lives. I had also become an ambassador for two other charities, The Brain Tumour Foundation of Canada and Cure Glioblastoma, based out of the United States, who were both doing boots-on-the-ground work at the research and funding level for glioblastoma.

But people were still dying alone. It wasn't enough. All the fundraised money in the world wouldn't matter if a caregiver couldn't access the person who needed the care. I was trying to give them money to buy them back some time. I was trying to alleviate their need to work or think or plan and gift them the opportunity to keep showing up for their parent or loved one. I went on a campaign and rallied over 100 people to write letters to our members of parliament, pleading for a better way to safely allow access for caregivers to family members in hospitals and long-term care facilities.

On May 29 of that same year, my mom's hospital reached out to me asking if I would come and do their first window visit – a new concept they were trying out where visitation with your loved one could be done with a window between you – them inside the building, you outside the building. It was working. I was being heard. I dreaded the idea of it though. I had not seen her in nearly two months and was terrified of how different she would look. My only contact had been FaceTimes but she was too confused and weak to operate a phone and so the nurse would hold it up for her and she would just stare past it.

The experience was unnerving. I took my kids and my brother, and we sat on the ground outside of a thick glass door. We chose sitting on the ground instead of standing because she was too weak to hold her head up. We got as low as we could instead. While ants crawled over our bare legs, we waved and blew kisses through the finger-smudged, pollen-dusted, glass. She had been wheeled right up to the door by a nurse. A triple layer of blankets slung across her lap, leaving us to only see the upper half of her, which look emaciated and gaunt. She was a shell.

She mostly never looked at us, but somewhere near or beside us as we awkwardly waved and spoke to no one. The chaplain chaperoning our outdoor visit left us with no privacy at all. (But luckily, more than willing to hold my phone and take all the pictures for me.)

In a moment near the end of our visit, as Richard and I said goodbye, the kids' attention span now challenged while they ran around starting a game of tag behind us, she shakily and slowly raised a hand to her face. We wondered if something was itching her. It appeared to be taking every ounce of energy she had to coordinate getting her hand up to her mouth. We watched her move in slow motion, hearts in our stomachs, wondering what she was doing. She finally found our eyes, somewhere in the process. She then found her mouth. But instead of scratching at something, she pressed the inside of her fingers to her lips and blew us a kiss. I wept, right there on the hard interlock pavers, ants on my legs, both hands pressed to the dirty glass.

Weeks later, in June, they opened again to try garden visits. This would now give family members the chance to visit in person, in the garden terrace, at a ten-feet distance, with masks, and no touching. I am not sure which was harder: being separated by two inches of thick, smudged glass, or being only ten feet away, separated by nothing but longing, and not being able to hug her.

Again, the hospital used me as their guinea pig. My voice was being heard and while my mom seemed to be the one reaping the benefits, so many other people would follow suit if I could follow the rules and show them that this would work. I did it. I did it ten times. Each one was no easier than the last. I remember the first visit, ironically, noticing ants crawling all over my mom, even across her neck, and having to call the supervising staff over from across the yard to wipe them off her. Doing it myself would have risked ending garden visits for not only myself but for everyone else as well.

Then finally, a few short weeks later, they opened the hospital back up to only caregivers for inside visits, still keeping a ten-foot distance and donning full PPE. Not great, but another step. We were getting there.

Late that summer things had opened slightly. Immediate family only was allowed in but it was predicted that another wave of COVID was coming for us, with the real threat of another round of hospital shutdowns coming. The vice president of the hospital reached out to me one day in July asking if I would help them create a program that would allow a designated caregiver to become an official part of the patient's care team, therefore ranking us as hospital staff and putting us in the circle with the doctors, nurses, and therapists. I could get back to my mom. Still in PPE, but no more ten-feet distance.

I jumped on board immediately and was thrust into

weekly meetings, round table discussions, protocols, agendas, and collaborations with different foundations around the province and country. I was their caregiving advocate. Finally, after weeks and weeks of deliberation and modifications, we were ready to roll out our Designated Care Partner Program, just in time for the second wave to hit us. We soft launched it at the hospital, ironically on my birthday, giving me twenty-four, seven access to my mom while the rest of the world was being shut out again for the second time in six months.

My mom's condition deteriorated drastically after this program launched, but I am blessed to have been such a big part of its planning and execution and blessed that it led me back to her. She did not endure a second wave of the pandemic isolated and truly alone.

A few weeks before I wrote this chapter, a friend, Jen, reached out to me to let me know that her stepmother was heading to St. Vincent's hospital that day to train in the Designated Care Partner program so that she could become her mother's caregiver. Jen thanked me for having been such a big part of initiating something like that so that so many people could benefit from it long after my mom had left, ensuring that a large part of my mother's legacy lived on.

You do not have to start a program or become an event planner to use the fuel. But you can do something. You can do so many things. Some days I literally used the fuel to power through a workout that I was not feeling in any way. I would think about my parents and a fight would build up inside of me that had me go from sluggish to grunting and sweating through a heavier weight than I had ever lifted before.

Make a post that brings awareness. Share someone else's post. Volunteer with a charity you believe in. Plan a small fundraiser like a garage sale. Donate a portion of your side gig paychecks for one month. (I donate 15 percent of my Beautycounter paychecks back to the Slay Society.) Donate something, somewhere, to someone. Attend a free webinar on the disease just to educate yourself, which in turn will help educate others. There are so many options, big and small. And by now, you probably do not need me to remind you what will happen to our frequency when you do good things.

You can choose whether you let the pain and the grief bury you alive and make you its victim for the rest of your life, or you decide to use it to propel you, your life, your cause, your purpose, forward. This does not mean that hard days will not exist. It sure does not mean that you are not honouring your parents. It means quite the opposite. It means that you can find purpose in pain. You can create something beautiful out of something ugly. You can rise from the ashes even though the ashes are still there. Pain and purpose, joy and heartache can co-exist.

Use your voice. Do not become a victim of circumstance but decide that you are going to give yourself the most empowering gift, speak up against it. Speak up despite it. Help others who are suffering silently. You can do that by not being one to suffer silently as well. Show that the light can be found if they are willing to step out of the darkness. In empowering others, you will empower yourself. Be the leader that my dad knows this world needs. Be the philanthropist and the heart that my mom embodied.

Because in the words of the song *Do Something* by Matthew West, "If not us, then who?"

12

GRIT AND GRACE

I wrote this book because I felt divinely guided through a journey that I sure did not want and never asked for. In the beginning, I panicked that I would not make it. I wondered how I was ever expected to care for two parents with matching GMB diagnoses and keep myself from having a mental breakdown. But I did it. And as I went along, I felt like I was being carried on the shoulders of so many incredible people. Fundraisers, meal trains, prayers, all lifted me from one hard day, one difficult moment, to the next. I continued to put one foot in front of the other carrying all those things in my heart as well as several well-worded and poignant mottos or quotes that became my mantras.

In the fall of 2017, I had joined Beautycounter. I never set out to find a multi-level marketing company but this one found me. I fell quickly in love with the fact that this company was mission-based – a movement. Their mission was to get safer products into the hands of everyone and their message was loud – change the face of the personal care industry. I knew that I needed to a part of this. I was all about living as cleanly as we could, ridding toxins that we could do without, et cetera. I jumped all in, feet first, and then immediately my feet froze. I was terrified to become "that girl" who was harassing everyone about her MLM business. I knew that, while those people do exist, I wasn't one of them. Nonetheless, the stigma is real, and I was struggling with how to get my message heard when people were generally just rolling their eyes at something they saw as a pyramid only. (Hint, all corporations and businesses are structured like a pyramid with management at the top. Do the math.)

I had this beautiful friend, Kimberly, a pastor, an advocate, an entrepreneur, a philanthropist, a fitness instructor, an all-around Oprah-like goddess warrior, who had started up a Beautycounter businesses at the same time and seemed to have far more people listening to her than I had. I messaged her one day pleading for a pep talk. How was she doing this? How did everyone seem to be taking her seriously while my family was tuning me out?

As it turned out, they were not all listening to her at all. She had just had the conversation with far more people than I had and by sheer statistics had caught more people's attention. She, unlike me, had not fallen victim to the self-questioning game that I had gotten stuck in. I was treading in a sea of self-pity that I was about to let swallow me whole, giving up on a business that was filling my cup.

Kim said to me, "You have to have two things, Laura: Grit and grace."

I knew immediately what she meant. I needed to have the grit to keep getting back up and not get discouraged, and the grace to know how to deliver my message with my head high. I used this little message to grow my business at the time but also applied it to my tumultuous journey of loving my parents through to the end of their lives.

I advocated loudly. I asked for help when needed. I accepted help when I did not ever think I could. I kept my head high. I openly shared sorrow. I found and shared joy. And I did it all unapologetically. I was not afraid to let the world know when I laughed or know when I just could not. By sharing in my journey, many people from all around the world reached out to share theirs, helping us all to feel so much less alone.

Learning to be loud without fear or judgment, with a dose of grit and grace, can serve you in two ways.

1. We live in a world where social media connects us all. To avoid sending 420 separate texts at every update, a post will unify everyone who genuinely cares for you, and them. Then watch the comments and loving energy flow in and bask in the supportive nature of it. You need it. You deserve it.
2. Those comments might just be what keeps you going. Your vulnerability and your strength, your grit and grace, will be commended, lifting you back up and showing other's the mountain that you are moving.

My dad said this to my mom on his first visit to see her in the hospital after her surgeries, his head still crowned with shiny metal staples, "Chris, it's like all of these people who have never met us are carrying us on their shoulders." I remember myself even saying that day that I felt like my feet had not touched the floor since day one of my dad being diagnosed because so many people were carrying me through it.

The realization of this, as I haven't talked about many times throughout this book, was supported by the realization that it was only because I was using my voice, being loud, open, and vulnerable, being seen, that so much support was coming in. Many people hide in the background or blend into the shadows in order to not draw attention to themselves, but that brings us back to the notion that fear only exists in the dark.

"We cultivate love when we allow our most vulnerable and powerful selves to be deeply seen and know."

— BRENÉ BROWN

I decided to use my grit, dig even deeper, and get even louder. Not because I needed more gift cards but because if people were finally listening then I could grab the stage in order to spread awareness about a disease so ruthless as to steal both of my parents from me simultaneously, one memory at a time. I saw an opportunity to speak loud and clear about glioblastoma, a terminal and incurable cancer that people know so little about.

The louder I got, the more people came out of the woodworks, hands raised, saying that they had lost someone to GBM as well. This rare cancer was not anywhere near as rare as we had thought. I concluded that it seemed so rare was because no one was talking about it. It is an unimaginably destructive disease leaving majority of people diagnosed not living past the first year. A small percentage live past three years. Therefore, there are few patients or survivors who can use their voice. Also, majority of GBM patients who have had their tumors surgically resected have done so with some deficits. Their speech, memory, brain function may be slightly impaired, hence, leaving them incapable of becoming spokespeople.

Caregivers are dragged through such a tumultuous experience that few come out of it with anything other than PTSD. I have seen many people leave glioblastoma support groups online and delete all GBM-related contacts or people they followed because the memories they were left with are simply too painful to relive or even think about. Few come through the journey with the capacity to keep talking about it or raising awareness and would much just like to forget that it all even happened (therefore, worsening their PTSD by the way).

This means that there is no one advocating. With every day that passed, I was shocked to find myself still standing on my two feet. I sometimes think that it was by the grace of God. Other times I think that it was the strength that my parents passed down to me. I sometimes wonder if it was mantras I had picked up along the way in life, like the gift of grit and grace from my beautiful friend Kimberly. *You need to have grit and grace, Laura.* I would hear myself tell myself: *If no one else is going to talk about this, you need to.*

And then there were the days where I would simply throw my hands in the air and wonder if it was honestly just because I had no other fucking choice. And neither do you. I always felt puzzled when people would say things like, "I don't know how you are doing this," or, "I wouldn't be able to do what you are doing." And I would just wonder what other choice I had. There was no way for me not to do what I was doing. My hands were tied. Your hands are tied. The cards have been dealt. You either play them with grit and grace or not at all. Ending my life would have been truly my other option in not facing their deaths. And it was not an option with three kids and a husband at home. Let alone a brother who was about to be orphaned with me and therefore needed me. And a community that I had built in the GBM world that counted on my advocacy, support and my loud, maybe only slightly annoying, voice. Although, the ending my life thing did cross my mind on several different occasions. Especially in the beginning when I wondered how I was supposed to go on and if maybe not going on at all would have been easier. I knew that I needed to change the face of GBM. Perhaps not necessarily the outcome, but the experience for its caregivers.

With all the grit and grace that I could muster, and the tools we have talked about in this book, I was able to become the caregiver that I ultimately wanted to be. The one that my parents truly deserved from me.

Now, the overwhelm can and will take over. There will be plenty of down and out days where the emotions, fear and pain are crippling. Part of the grace piece is giving that grace to yourself. Giving yourself the grace to feel the feelings, take the breaks, sneak away to cry, lower your expectations, is imperative to your mental health. A lot is going to be asked of you as a caregiver. Remember that you have been called to do God's work and you will be struggling with letting go of pieces of them in the process. It is not a sprint. However, you may feel like you want to do it all. Clear your schedule and make room for calm. You cannot dig deep if the cup is empty.

Here is a beautiful visual and metaphor that I took a lot of value from these past years. Imagine yourself as a large glass vase. As caregivers (this is commonly used specifically for moms and women but let's do caregiver for the sake of this exercise), we tend to want to take all of our goodness and give it to those we love, particularly our dying parent or loved one. Imagine that all the goodness out there like love, hydration, gifts, self-care, nutrition, reading, sports, crafting, art, therapy, girls' nights, guys nights, hugs, laughter, – to name a few – imagine that all those things are water pouring into your vase all day long. What do you notoriously do as a selfless, love-giving being? You constantly tip yourself over, trying to give a little bit of all that goodness away to the people around us. You tip over and pour into your kids, your spouses, your friends. What happens if you are a glass vase always tipping over and pouring into other people, bending wildly at all angles? You *will* eventually tip over. Shatter. Break.

What if you stood tall and unwavering? What if you kept your head up and your shoulders back? What if, for once, you let all that goodness just pour into you at a steady stream and stopped dumping it out? It would come in, fill you up, all the way to the tippity top until you overflowed. That's right. You would overflow all that love, light, laughter out of yourself and it would naturally fall into all the cups around you, filling them up to their tops too.

Let the cup, the vase, the wonderful you, fill up. Then when you need to dig deep – and there will be so many times – you have an endless depth of goodness to take from. Find the grit to keep going and the grace to let the goodness pour in so that you can let all the beautiful magic pour over and drench them in the love they need.

13

THE FINAL DRAGON

It was a Monday morning. October 19, 2020. I got the kids successfully to school, not without a tantrum thrown in somewhere, somehow – likely by me. I gave myself the morning to quietly catch up on work and decided to push my visit with my mom closer to lunch. The phone rang. It was my mom's nurse. She sounded small and quiet, like she was afraid of her next words. There had a been a change, she told me. My mom had become too weak and too tired to open her eyes, eat, or take any of her medications. It was my mom's time to go. This would be the end.

I dropped my work and headed straight there. I was sick again at the idea of the inevitable events that I knew would follow this day. I had done this already once, only six short months ago.

The yellow walls, the drabness, the sadness, it had all become a grossly familiar part of me. It had encased the last of my relationship with my mother. My ability to love her fully would always be backdropped by this yellow, these stains, this smell, this gut-churning feeling. And yet, I did not want it to end.

I rushed straight to her room on shaky legs and with a twitching heart and found her exactly the way the nurse had described her – nearly lifeless. Increasingly, over the past few weeks, her eyes would open less and less often. Standing there in that moment, I knew that I would not be privileged with seeing them again. As grey as they had become, they still felt like home. But this was one more small piece I would have to let go of as I made my way to a full goodbye, one more part of her crossed off the list.

I sat and cried beside her, knowing that finally, after so many close calls, so many declines and unexpected ascends, so many practice goodbyes and long walks out of her room and back down the hallway, this one was for real.

I made the decision with her nurse and her doctor to end the medications and let her go.

I then let Marc and Richard know that it was time to come in. We would not get the gift of knowing the preciseness of how many days or hours were left. You never do. We were told one to two with my dad, and we got nine. We knew by now that it could be a long week and we, all three, were prepared to set up camp and stay until there was no more of her to stay with.

I, once again, arranged for friends to pick up the kids from school each day that week. I then marched straight into the manager's office and demanded a private room. If we were going to say goodbye, we sure were not going to do it beside a patient with dementia who was constantly half-naked or ripping our curtains open or asking me how I like the dinner her brain was telling her she had just prepared and served me (as lovely as she was.) Nor was I going to allow myself to be left in a room with three other men in the middle of the night while discovering that my parent was no longer breathing. They moved her within the hour. Most of the city knew, at this point, that my family and I had suffered enough, and most were willing to move mountains for us if they could.

Her room was still yellow, still drab, still full of the whispering sadness of lives entering and lives ending. But it had a big window, and it was private. I took care transferring and arranging her joy-inducing-plants, and then took equal care-taking half of her belongings and throwing them in the garbage. It seemed heartless, to literally toss things like nail clippers, shirts and sympathy cards into the trash can below the sink of her old room, but I needed the end to feel like the end and knew that I would be in no place to be burdened by material stuff later. What she needed now was love. For love is all that matters.

And so, it would go that for five more days we would circle back to the routine of sleeping on stiff, narrow hospital chair beds. (The use of the word "beds" for hospitals everywhere should seriously be called into question.) We would pop back home for breaks only to suffer panic attacks on the drive, more panic attacks while home, decide we could not take the panic attacks, change our plan, and come back to her room early. Being away was harder than watching her go.

COVID in Ottawa was still in a dire place being in its second wave. St. Vincent's hospital was in its own outbreak, the worst the city had seen within a hospital thus far. However, by some sort of cosmic alignment, we were able to have four people in her room at a time, making this round feel much more beautiful and even slightly less scary than my dad's. Perhaps this time I would not be alone.

There was something inside me that, once again, desired beyond words to be the one that was there when they took their final breaths.

Social media post: date unknown.

"I wanted it to be me. Even though it terrified me, I

wanted with all of my heart to be the one who would be next to them when they exhaled for the last time."

Whether I wanted it so badly that I somehow manifested it, or they wanted it to and waited for me, I'll never know. But it happened twice.

It was the twenty-third of October, I woke up from my bed of chairs. It had become a treat, having that stupid rock-hard bed of chairs as the previous night I had given Marc the reclining sleeper chair and resorted to just lining up a few chairs and lying across them, my feet dangling wildly off the end, tingling until they would wake me up.

Two nights before, the nurses had snagged me a proper reclining sleeper chair from another room. *Probably a room where someone had just died*, I thought. The thought made me uneasy, but I was too tired to give that thought much space so happily curled up into my hoodie, threw a paper-thin hospital sheet over myself and lay there again, cold, and uncomfortable, wondering if my rigged-up chair line had been a better idea. Turned out in the end that I was right. The recliner did not recline much at all and sleeping in an upright position was not working for me. The next night I went back to my tried-and-true method of lining up three hard plastic chairs and laying across them. I may have lost all feeling in my feet, but I was at least horizontal.

Marc had spent every single night there that week. I had tried a few nights at home but ended up regretting each one, spending every twenty minutes rolling over to check my phone in case I had missed a text from him, then assuming that my notifications had been turned off so opened my phone and opened my text app and each time, finding nothing other than my increased level of angst.

Neither of us had slept when we finally started moving and stretching our bodies that Friday morning. She seemed different. For days she had looked tense, sullen, suffering.

Her mouth had gaped open some days before and remained that way. Her body had looked stiff all week. No matter what we did to relax her neck and jaw, close her mouth, it would fall open again shortly after. Her breathing had been loud and growing increasingly louder, sometimes stopping altogether before she would gasp again. Chain stocking, they called it, which I had already learned from my fresh end-of-life experience with my dad – an end-of-life sign.

None of these things scared me anymore, the way they had with him. The mottling in her legs, the gasps for air, the eyes shooting open as if something had startled them, (their parents standing by, arms outstretched, waiting and welcoming, I imagined), the noisy exhales, the tremors, they had all become a familiar part of the end-of-life experience that I was building my expertise in.

With the hospital having allowed us four visitors at a time, much of our week was beautifully spent with her brothers, big and little, as well as a small fleury of nieces, sisters-in-law and friends. It was happening, ending, the way it was supposed to. It was all the things my dad had been robbed of.

On that morning, her last morning, she seemed different – peaceful. Her mouth was closed. This was the first thing I noticed when I rose that morning and looked up from my low-to-the-ground bed of chairs beside her. Her mouth was closed and soft. Her breathing was rhythmic and soft. Her hands looked relaxed and soft. There was a sudden softness that was visible, palpable. It put Marc and me immediately at ease.

The sun was shining brilliantly out of her big fifth-floor, south-facing window. The artistically arranged plants that I had given so much care to were thriving and basking in the warmth. I pulled the curtains fully open so that we could feel the same. *How comforting would it be for her to feel the sun kissing her skin?* I wondered. And then, just like that, my brain did a 180-degree turn and I wondered if she was making a turn for the better. Was she rallying? Could she be doing this again? Leaving us broken and on edge, awaiting, all week long just to pull through and make a comeback? Could she beat this? Walk out of this place like so many others do not?

I wondered if Marc thought the same. He was not one to roll his eyes at miracles. His Christian faith would have him holding onto one until the last second. But his mind must have been following a similar trajectory as mine because he suddenly spoke up, breaking my miracle-guided trance, and said, "It looks beautiful out there. I think I will step out and go for a walk later. Get some fresh air."

Marc and I had a strained relationship at the best of times. His drinking and my overprotective possessiveness of my mother were never a good match. In many moments, our time together, over their seventeen-year marriage, felt forced. In others it came more naturally. But never when there was alcohol. Until eventually, there was so much alcohol that I decided there was no more time together.

Now, for several months, he had remained sober. No doubt finding the strength in his adoration for his wife and his adamant desire to make her proud. The one wish she had in the past seventeen years was for Marc to save himself. "God is still in the miracle business, Laura." She would faithfully remind me, eyes full of hope, as a counter to me encouraging her to finally leave him and put herself first, for once.

But now, unlike in the beginning of our big, demented, blended family's dual diagnoses journey, he had made good on his promise to be the man she knew he could be. He had certainly earned the right to feel good about that.

It's a hard thing – grief. You are going to see quickly that your sibling, friend, stepparent, or even other parent, will handle and approach things so incredibly different than you. Part of the mastery of moving through this time successfully, is not judging each other for our grief.

Marc's way and my way were different. He was dealing with the illness of an addiction. I was not. He was about to lose his wife and be left in a house alone. I still had a husband and three loving kids in mine. These stories about him are not to slander him in any way. They are a way to reach any one of you who may be reading this book as an addict, or with an addict, and to show you that you are not alone. I also felt this was a beautiful way to show you how Marc truly pulled through in the end; how he triumphantly rose above the thing that had been pulling him down most of his adult life, and he did it for the love of his life. His life will go forward without my mom and his heart will be forever fractured because of it. But in the final moments, right down to the bell and hopefully more after, he was able to hold on to her, her life, her heart, and her hands, with full sobriety and clarity. You cannot buy that kind of feeling. I watched it with my eyes.

We sat, the two of us having somehow reversed sleeping chairs, folded back up from bed to seating. It was approaching 10:00 a.m. We flanked my mom's hospital bed, facing each other, and talked the morning away while she slept. He shared stories of his childhood, offering up a much more vulnerable side of himself than I had seen in a long time, maybe ever. I was connecting with sober Marc. *This is nice*, I smiled at the thought. I assumed that my mom could hear everything. She must have been basking in the warmth of the room, not just from the sun beams hugging her skin but from the contended energy of our story sharing and laughing. The fact that for once, she likely felt in me a level of acceptance that I had not been able to find in a long while.

We sat like that, chatting, and laughing, reminiscing, and

smiling, holding her hands, and interlacing our fingers with hers, for hours. *Is this it, Mom? Is this what you been waiting for all this time? Here we are, being a family.*

And just then, just like that, as if answering my question, she softly gasped for air. Her breathing took a sudden shift into an unfamiliar shallowness. This time I did not have to be alone. Marc looked up at me through worried eyes and said, "Actually, I don't think I am going to go for a walk."

"No," I agreed. "I don't think you should."

We pulled our chairs closer to the bed, knees crunched against the rail. We held her hands and watched her, wondering what to do, who to call, what to say. I pulled my phone out and propped it up against my mom's left hip, assuming she would not mind. Gripping her hand with my right, I used my left to try to text my brother. I only needed to write a few words but with my non-dominant hand, it proved challenging. "Come. I think it's happening," was as much as I could manage.

I am not sure if you believe in angels, but I do. A woman, Lorraine, had appeared in the hallway weeks earlier as I donned my PPE outside of my mom's room one day. She had come up to me with eyes sparkling and I imagine a face-splitting, mile-wide smile, only I could not see it under her mask and face shield. She was small in stature but made up for it in exuberance.

"Oh, you are Christine's daughter," she clapped as she approached me. I recognized a thick French accent. I wondered if I had met her before and flushed with guilt for forgetting. "I'm Lorraine. We haven't met." *Oh, thank God.* "I am a support worker here and I just love your mom. I am so excited to meet you. I told her that if she had a daughter that she must be as special as she is. I connect with her so much and just love spending time with her."

She got all of that from a woman who had not even been able to speak for three months?

Lorraine, whom I immediately would have described as a ball of light, and I became fast friends. I loved her for my mom. Whoever had sent her here, I thanked God that she found her way to my mom's room.

In that moment when my mom's breathing changed, I quickly excused myself to run to the bathroom. If she was going to hold on for anything longer than thirty minutes, I did not want to suffer through my last moments with her on a full bladder. She deserved for me to be fully present. But for that, I would need to pee. I squeezed her hand and told her not to go anywhere. I ran to the washroom and ran into Lorraine on my hurried way back. I had not seen Lorraine yet that day, but she had been in visiting every other day that week. She would sit beside my mom and stroke her hair and sing softly to her or pray over her. She stopped me to ask how my mom was and I just looked at her with a deadpan face and said, "I think this is it. It's happening right now."

All the color in Lorraine's petite body drained to her petite shoes.

"Do you want to come and say goodbye?" I asked. "I would love for you to."

There was no hesitation, not even a fraction of a second's worth. Lorraine just turned on her heels and followed me in. And then we were three.

I reclaimed my seat as Lorraine took up standing room only at my mom's head. She went right back to stroking her hair and running her hand along her forehead. I relatched onto my mom's hand and frantically checked to see if Richard had gotten back to me. "Fuck. For real?" read the banner that flashed across my screen.

"Hurry," I replied.

Richard did not particularly want to be there. He did not

want to see her passing, for reasons of his own, and it had taken me a while to learn that we were all different. He didn't have the desire to have that be his last memory. Whereas I believed it may bring me more closure to see it all the way through. He texted again that he was on his way.

"Keep breathing, okay Mom? Rich is coming."

My heart started fluttering. The nerves and the panic were starting to set in. This was it. My final goodbye. My last chance. A chance that many do not get but then a chance that I wonder if many could handle. My heart further breaking, minute by minute, shallow breath by shallow breath.

Lorraine suddenly asked if she had a rosary. I almost rolled my eyes at the inquiry. Of course, she had a rosary. Her sister had brought her one when she first entered St. Vincent's. She had used it more as a fidget toy than she was able to pray with it but now was its time to shine. I snatched it from the bedside table, wrapped it around her hands, and wrapped my hand around hers. We leaned over her, watching every breath. The long pauses in between felt like an eternity. We decided on music. This was Marc's thing. I read to her. He played music and sang to her. It felt like the most perfect thing for this moment. "Quick, Marc, name a song." I frantically requested. He did not waver, *How Many Kings* he blurted out, eyes rimming with tears.

Within moments we had her favorite song playing, but still no Richard. The tears and hurt were increasing as the song went on. With every note, I squeezed her frail hand harder. Then, I felt the love wash over me, overtake me. For all the things she had given me ... all the things she had taught me ... all the gifts she had left me with ... how would I say enough thank you with the mere moments I had left?

I squeezed my eyes shut and pressed the back of her hand into my forehead, rosary wrapped in her palm, cross dancing and swaying between us. I stood, leaned over, and kissed her forehead just as the last note of the song faded to an end. And with that, she drew one small breath, then was gone.

With the same quiet softness with which she would have cradled me in her arms as a babe and whispered me a lullaby, she slipped out of this world and onto the next, where my dad was waiting to greet her.

The lesson is that we are not guaranteed time. I loved them through their deaths instead of turning away from them with fear, which is the only reason I can walk away without regrets, for it is love that matters most.

THE LESSONS WE LEARN

"You can't go back and change the beginning, but you can start where you are and change the ending."

— C.S. LEWIS

You now have the tools needed to face your caregiving journey with your head high, knowing that you have left no regrets. You have learned what it means to love someone until the end. You should now have a new comfort level with the topic of death and dying and will be able to empower other caregivers going forward. You will be able to walk through their journey with newfound strength and purpose. Here is a recap of where we have been together:

Breathe In, Breathe Out

No matter how difficult a moment may feel, allow yourself the simple pleasure of breathing. And remember that you can do hard things. Start and end your day with ten controlled deep breaths to slow your heart rate and fill your body with oxygen.

Practice several different breathing techniques to find the one that works best for you. Remember that there may be moments so overwhelming that it will be all you can do to remind yourself to breathe in and breathe out. You cannot change what the situation is, but you can change how you, even how they, experience it.

Play the Part

One of the most important ways in which not to lose yourself will be putting your basic health needs at the top of your priority list. And yes, I know how hard this can seem. But the truth is, it is not difficult. They are labelled "basic" needs for a reason – we cannot survive without them. What kind of caregiver would you be if you cannot even remember to nourish yourself?

Find a realistic and attainable way to prioritize yourself in order to move forward in optimal mental and physical health. The simplest things, like hydrating, will help you prevent a myriad of other health problems, both physical and mental, and help you stay together even when you do not feel like you are.

I will say it again – remember that you are doing God's work here. Would you mistreat Him, or for that matter, the hospital staff, if He were here in person lovingly caring for your parent? No, you would likely thank Him and keep Him cared for. Now that you are playing that part give yourself that same love and respect.

Get Organized

We talked about the importance of organizing your priorities. Notice here that I did not say "life?" Let's accept that life is going to look a whole lot different and trying to live the same normal you were living before might not be the best approach. If you are feeling more overwhelmed than you'd ever thought possible, and a simple daily decision – such as which latte to try as you stare at the menu board, hordes of impatient, caffeine-deficient people in line behind you – has you nearly bursting into tears and running away screaming (I have been there) then perhaps you are already taking on too much and it is time for a to-do list revamp. Prioritize minimally with simple task-oriented lists, delegate certain to-dos, and let go of the extra. You are living in crisis mode. Embrace it.

And in case you neglected to get this done between Chapter 6 and here, I will offer another reminder with all the love I can muster for you: Get your damn will done. (Or theirs.)

Create Your Environment.

It is imperative that you create a healing environment for yourself by blocking out energy suckers, choosing joy, and accepting help. Put yourself in your parent's shoes. You likely went out and bought extra throw blankets in case they are cold at chemo (because you heard that happens). You probably picked up a big, overstuffed ottoman for them to elevate their feet when they are home resting from treatments. (I did). And do not try to tell me that you or someone you know did not load them up on sudoku, crosswords, gossip magazines, and scratch tickets. (Guilty again.) Did you also load the fridge with healthy, iron-loaded packages of prewashed spinach and more vitamin-C-rich fruit than they have likely ever consumed in their lifetime? Yeah, you did.

Would you go head-to-head with anyone that even thought about bringing negativity into their life at this point? (Tell Sheila to take a hike.) And if someone offered to cook them a meal, would you politely decline that offer on their behalf? Fuck no. You would revel at the thought and the love that poured from someone else all over your mom or dad (or insert loved one) because you know they need it.

You tried to create for them a healing environment. Give yourself that same love. You are going to need it if you are now leading the charge.

Lose the Fear

That load of fear you were toting around of providing physical and emotional care for them, it is gone. And thank the good lord because it was heavy. Wasn't it? By Educating yourself on the disease you are dealing with, its medical terms, as well as proper support work techniques, you are much better equipped to step in when something difficult, uncomfortable, or even scary, comes up. Sign up for any free classes or webinars you can. And when you can, take them as you sit presently, alongside your parent, while they sleep peacefully or watch you as you empower yourself to kick ass.

Now that you have realized that you are their biggest advocate you can use that voice of yours to become one with their care team. Get cozy and acquainted. As long as you don't become an overbearing pain in the ass, most nurses and doctors appreciate family or caregiver support more than we realize. They are spread thin, there are not always enough of them to go around. And while we can argue all day that your parent's care is never going to be as important to them as it is to you, most people who walk willingly into a career of needle prodding and bum wiping are not doing it because they lack empathy. They care. Be willing to work with them. Together, with your strengths and input, you can work toward creating the best possible care for your parent. Imagine how loved they must feel now?

The Self-Care Myth

Now that you have identified your go-to list of self-care, you have hopefully put those techniques into practice and are feeling much more like yourself. When challenges increase, you have an arsenal of go-to tricks to help bring your feet back to the ground, or to get them back underneath you, whichever way you want to look at it. You are doing this one minute at a time. And when those minutes string together in threads of more relaxed time and space, you can breathe, bathe, get outdoors, throw yourself a party, whatever your new, for now, mojo has become.

I used to hate it, and still do if we are being completely honest, when people would say to me, "What would your parents want you to do?" I used to go through snarky responses in my head such as, *Easy for you to say. Who cares what they would want, they are leaving me and then I have to live with the rest.* Or my favourite but certainly not shiniest or most mature thoughts, *They would probably* not *want me to throat punch you right now.*

But it is true, isn't it? We are not living our lives to fully please our parents. We should not be anyway. There are plenty of other books on that that you should move on to next if that is what you are doing. But they, without a shadow of a doubt, *do* want you to take care of yourself. Always and forever. They love you enough to want that for you. Love yourself enough to love yourself too.

Dig Deep

Picture my dad, all 185 pounds of his squashed 5 feet 8 inches frame, yelling and cheering this from the sidelines of the proverbial soccer field to you. Or if it would help you to insert an image of your parent, feel free to replace mine. (But he is kind of awesome.)

You have learned to listen and embrace your difficult emotions in order to move through them with resiliency. And that, my friend, is not an easy thing to accomplish. Pat yourself on the back if you feel that you have made great strides. And if you are still too scared of your feeling-filled shadow, be patient with yourself and keep at it. There are going to be a lot of jumbled feelings to feel here. This work is not for the faint of heart.

I encourage you to keep working at it while you still have the time to do so. You can do this. You can do those hard things, remember? Start with a letter. Even if you just leave it with them, it is a step that you will be forever grateful you took.

But if nothing else, say "I love you." Love transcends. Love can conquer all.

Use the Fuel

You are now an empowered advocate and carry with you the magic and the power to make change while creating a legacy for your parent. And this legacy thing, this will be the absolute best way to keep them alive and with you forever and ever. This is giving a purpose not only to you but to a disease, an illness, a circumstance that did not quite make sense before. It may still not make any damn sense on its own, but you have the upper hand in creating sense in an area where there was none before.

Believe me when I say that I would trade my charity back for two healthy, vibrant parents on this earth. But the love they left me has birthed a legacy for them that no one will ever undo. Their light will shine brighter now than it ever could have before. They need me to do this work. They wanted me to do this work. And I love them enough to not let them down.

Your work may not be building a charity that will help thousands, maybe even millions one day. Your work could be to teach and pass down the lessons they left you to your children. Whatever it is, use this as fuel to propel yourself toward it. The love is fuel and fuel is the love. Let the love strengthen you enough to move that mountain.

Do it with grit. Do it with grace. Do it while you allow the love from the outside to pour into you so that you can spill it out onto everyone around you. Then think about how much you have filled the heart of the person you are giving yours to.

You have made me proud my incredible caregiving friend. You had better be proud of yourself too. This is God's work, and you are doing it. with that, consider yourself up there with some of the best, the mentally strongest, and most bad-ass powerful people out there. Use that love and go forward with your head up, shoulders back, walking forward.

You are slaying dragons.

ACKNOWLEDGMENTS

Here is a page that I feel I could start and never end. I am overflowed with gratitude when I even begin think about the love and support I've received since day one of a diagnosis that would shake up my world. I will do my best to give energy and thanks to the people who have stood behind me, but I know that I will never be able to write about everyone or there will need to be a second book published.

My husband, Kenny, who stands silently behind me, no matter my endeavor, triumphantly holding down the fort, holding up our family and holding on to a steady job and paycheck without the ego or expectation.

Leightyn, Ryann, and Wesley, my most prized possessions. You have seen more in your early childhood than many people see in a lifetime. You have had to learn big lessons early and have done it with grit and grace. Thank you for letting me be your mom. I pray that you will always love me the same way that I loved my own.

My brother, Richard, who when I asked flat out whether I should just jump in, invest the money, and write this book, answered with a resounding "Yes" and has never stopped believing that I could do just about anything.

My best mama friends, Colleen, Corissa, and Melissa, who have spent endless hours picking up my kids after school, loving them, feeding them, entertaining them, while I lived in hospitals. And who have since spent as many endless hours in back and forth conversations with me hashing out details of my book. You have always been there to listen or offer advice and have held more space for me than anyone else in this world. I love all three of you.

Jessica, for whom I wrote this book. My love letter from one caregiver to another. The things I would say to you if we were sitting in a café, face to face, are in these chapters. This book was written with you in my heart, your beautiful face in my mind, your fragile heart in my hands. I know that you can do this. Thank you for allowing me the opportunity to put it into words.

My cousin Jamie, without whom I would not have survived many of the moments of the past two years. You always know the exact right time to show up. And that is not by coincidence. I love you as a sister and although we will never get the mother daughter trip we had planned for a dreamed of, we will get somewhere together someday, and my mom, your aunt, will no doubt be present. Thank you for keeping me standing.

My childhood best friends, Kristy, Jen, and Sandra, thank you for loving me so unconditionally that in the moments when I became a soap box star or a preaching professional, you looked past that, understood me and loved my anyways. You all possess a superpower called loyalty and I am so blessed to have done more than thirty years of life with each of you.

To all my followers and supporters who have observed the craziness unfold over the past two years with nothing but support and empathy. For all of you who have taken the time to read the posts, cry with me, cheer with me, fight with me, and ever write the words, "You should write a book.", thank you.

My beautiful sparkly soul of an editor, Cory. You kept me smiling and giggling all the way through the process. Thank you for having the patience with me when I needed to push dates and ask all the questions and for understanding, without knowing, that life in a pandemic with three kids virtual learning, while working two jobs and running a charity wasn't the most ideal environment to be writing a book in and yet, here we are. I did it. We did it. And we only got here because of your compassion and talents. I would write one thousand books with you.

Lastly, although I could go on forever, I want to acknowledge, thank, give praise to, and shout out so fucking loud to Angela Lauria and the entire team at The Author Incubator. Thank you for seeing something in me that would lead you to believe that I could write this book. Thank you for coaching me all the way through and allowing me to develop into an entirely new, shinier, and more self-aware form of myself; one that you already knew existed.

ABOUT THE AUTHOR

Laura Dill is a caregiving coach in Ottawa, Canada, where she lives with her incredibly supportive husband, Kenny, and their three energetic children. Her life as a horticulturist and landscape designer took a drastic turn at the end of 2019 when her parents were both diagnosed with incurable brain cancer only fourteen days apart.

Laura went from a fast-paced landscaping business owner to full-time caregiver as quickly as the diagnosis was uttered. She dedicated herself to caring for her parents, determined to help them live out their days with no regrets, full of love joy and laughter, all while trying to balance mom life, entrepreneurial life, and married life. She quickly discovered though that the biggest challenge would be learning how to do it all without falling apart herself.

While every pillar around her seemed to crumble, and the days her parents had left seemed to dwindle, a global pandemic was dropped into the mix, leaving Laura and the rest of her family isolated from two dying parents in hospitals.

Laura has fought to help the hospital develop a caregiver partnership program that would allow her back to her mother, while also creating a charity based on her father's favourite and timely motto, "Slay one dragon at a time," that would provide financial and emotional support for fellow caregivers of glioblastoma.

Since losing both parents in 2020, Laura has helped hundreds of people with the intention of reaching so many more with her book. By sharing her story, she is determined to show others that loving somebody to the end of their life is the only way to thrive through a journey so unimaginably heart-wrenching that it would otherwise take you down. She is sharing the strategies and coping mechanisms that she discovered, through trial and error, kept her going forward when she feared that she would never find the strength to stand back up.

She is here to show you that no matter how heart-breaking your path is, you can do it and get to the other side of it with love. For love is all that matters.

ABOUT DIFFERENCE PRESS

Difference Press is the exclusive publishing arm of The Author Incubator, an educational company for entrepreneurs – including life coaches, healers, consultants, and community leaders – looking for a comprehensive solution to get their books written, published, and promoted. Its founder, Dr. Angela Lauria, has been bringing to life the literary ventures of hundreds of authors-in-transformation since 1994.

A boutique-style self-publishing service for clients of The Author Incubator, Difference Press boasts a fair and easy-to-understand profit structure, low-priced author copies, and author-friendly contract terms. Most importantly, all of our #incubatedauthors maintain ownership of their copyright at all times.

LET'S START A MOVEMENT WITH YOUR MESSAGE

In a market where hundreds of thousands of books are published every year and are never heard from again, The Author Incubator is different. Not only do all Difference

Press books reach Amazon bestseller status, but all of our authors are actively changing lives and making a difference.

Since launching in 2013, we've served over 500 authors who came to us with an idea for a book and were able to write it and get it self-published in less than six months. In addition, more than 100 of those books were picked up by traditional publishers and are now available in bookstores. We do this by selecting the highest quality and highest potential applicants for our future programs.

Our program doesn't only teach you how to write a book – our team of coaches, developmental editors, copy editors, art directors, and marketing experts incubate you from having a book idea to being a published, best-selling author, ensuring that the book you create can actually make a difference in the world. Then we give you the training you need to use your book to make the difference in the world, or to create a business out of serving your readers.

ARE YOU READY TO MAKE A DIFFERENCE?

You've seen other people make a difference with a book. Now it's your turn. If you are ready to stop watching and start taking massive action, go to http://theauthorincubator.com/apply/.

"Yes, I'm ready."

OTHER BOOKS BY DIFFERENCE PRESS

Skinny Genes: The Surprising Truth about Every Body's Capacity to Settle at a Natural Weight, Even When Diets Have Failed by Arianne Bozarth, CNS, MS

Family Business Legacy Plan: The Ultimate Guide to Creating a Legacy for Your Family without Paying too Much in Taxes by Maria L. Ellis, MBA

iMove: Helping Your Clients Heal from Compulsive Exercise by Amy Gardner, MS, CERD, RYT

Rising Beyond Betrayal: One Woman's Quest for Peace after Tragedy, Trauma, and Loss by Lise-Marie Monroe

The Business of Essential Oils: A Heart-Centered Entrepreneur's Guide to Adding a New Stream of Revenue by Lori Rothschild, PhD

True Gifts: Ignite Your Soul Magic and Monetize the Highest Expression of Your Purpose by Jewel Veitch

No More Playing Small: Free Your Inner Rockstar and Go All in on Your Full-Time Coaching Career by Megan Jo Wilson

THANK YOU

From my mending heart to yours:

I want to tell you how grateful I am to you, my reader, for taking the time out of your life, journey, process, to take a step into mine. While I hate that any of this may have resonated with you, my hope is that the reality of our connection brings you peace of mind knowing that you are not, never have been, and never will be alone in your fight.

I know firsthand the gift of time on this earth. For you to graciously allow me enough of yours to walk this journey with me has not only meant to world to me but allowed me to show my parents, watching over us, that their plight will never be in vain. Their lessons and legacy continue.

Please share your caregiving wins and struggles with me on IG @lauradill12 in order to help me be the best caregiving coach I can be.

And please follow the Slay Society on Instagram @slaysocietyinc or on Facebook @slaysociety to help us support caregivers and raise awareness for Glioblastoma.

Use your time and make it all count.

For being here for them and being here for yourself, I love you and you should too.

Made in the USA
Middletown, DE
05 August 2021

45460741R00116